A WOMAN WHO DOESN'T QUIT

5 Habits

FROM THE BOOK OF RUTH

Nicki Koziarz

LifeWay Press® Nashville, Tennessee

Published by LifeWay Press®

© 2016 Nicki Koziarz

Reprinted October 2020

No part of this book may be reproduced or transmitted in any form or by any means, electronic or mechanical, including photocopying and recording, or by any information storage or retrieval system, except as may be expressly permitted in writing by the publisher. Requests for permission should be addressed in writing to LifeWay Press®; One LifeWay Plaza; Nashville, TN 37234-0152.

ISBN 9781430051534 • Item 005772638

Dewey decimal classification: 248.843

Subject headings: PERSEVERANCE / BIBLE. O.T. RUTH / WOMEN

Unless otherwise noted, Scripture quotations are taken from the Holman Christian Standard Bible®, Copyright © 1999, 2000, 2002, 2003, 2009 by Holman Bible Publishers. Used by permission. Holman Christian Standard Bible®, Holman CSB®, and HCSB® are federally registered trademarks of Holman Bible Publishers. Scripture quotations marked NIV are taken from the Holy Bible, NEW INTERNATIONAL VERSION®. Copyright © 1973, 1978, 1984 by Biblica, Inc. All rights reserved worldwide. Used by permission. Scripture quotations marked NLT are taken from the Holy Bible, New Living Translation, Copyright © 1996. Used by permission of Tyndale House Publishers, Inc., Wheaton, IL 60189 USA. All rights reserved. Scripture quotations marked MSG are taken from The Message. Copyright © 1993, 1994, 1995, 1996, 2000, 2001, 2002. Used by permission of NavPress Publishing Group.

To order additional copies of this resource, write to LifeWay Church Resources Customer Service; One LifeWay Plaza; Nashville, TN 37234-0113; fax 615.251.5933; phone 800.458.2772; email *orderentry@lifeway.com*; or order online at *www.lifeway.com*.

Printed in the United States of America

Cover design The Visual Rep

Adult Ministry Publishing
LifeWay Church Resources • One LifeWay Plaza • Nashville, TN 37234-0152

Contents

Nicki Koziarz

is an author and speaker with Proverbs 31 Ministries. Each week she helps thousands of women through P31 Online Bible Studies. She and her husband, Kris, own a fixer-upper farm just outside Charlotte, North Carolina. There they are raising their three beautiful (but hormonal) daughters, a barnyard of misfit animals, and one slightly famous pug. After a broken experience in the church, Nicki is consumed with learning to lead her generation on the pursuit of Truth and Love.

Introduction

IS THERE SOMETHING YOU ARE READY TO QUIT?
IS THERE SOMEONE YOU WANT TO GIVE UP ON?

Perseverance is one of the greatest skills but one of the hardest lessons we will learn in our lifetime. We are living in a day when we are encouraged to do life based on how we feel.

I want to eat what I want to eat, but stay healthy.

I want to follow God, but only if it feels good.

I want to serve others, but, if I don't feel like it, I tell myself there's always another day.

Every now and then I'll get an ounce of determination and start to pursue the dreams, the talents, and the gifts God has given me with all my might, but it seems like once I get going, something is always trying to stop me.

I often quit before I even realize I've quit.

Maybe you can relate.

You bombed the interview and didn't get the job you wanted, so you gave up trying and settled for the other position.

The first run you went on left you on the side of the road throwing up, so you never ran again.

A business you started failed, so you threw in the towel of entrepreneurship.

Marriage got messy, complicated, and hard, so you stopped trying.

I'm not proud to own this title, but I truly am the quitting expert. All those things above *and more* have been part of my quitting journey.

But then I discovered this woman in the Bible, Ruth, and she taught me so much more than a Bible story. Through her life I uncovered five life-giving habits to help me persevere when things get hard, complicated, and messy.

These habits do more than just motivate me—they help me to fight resistance when it rises. They've taught me to pursue discipline instead of desire as I determine my daily direction.

I've learned the direction of our lives needs to be far less about to-do lists and accomplishments but more about becoming people God can count on.

And when we become someone God can count on, incredible things start to happen. Lives are transformed, generational lines of bondage are broken, and we become the best possible version of ourselves.

The enemy of our souls, Satan, knows what pushes us to our limits. He wants us to give up on the hopes, dreams, and plans God has for us. He wants you to quit because then there is one less threat to him.

There is power when women come together and call Satan out on his arrows of defeat.

We will not be women who back down from the promises of God. We will not let fear keep us from pushing through. And when that day comes and we stand before our God, He will say,"Well done, my good and faithful servant" (Matt. 25:21, NLT).

Yes, friend, we can and will do hard things (together).

HOW THIS WILL WORK

I know your life's complicated, busy, and challenging. The last thing I want you to do is quit your Bible study! I'm keeping things as simple as possible for you to be successful through this study.

Each week you'll come together with hopefully at least one other person to discuss, challenge each other, and study the Book of Ruth together. You have the option to watch a short video teaching each week as well!

- The person/group I'm studying this with is _____.
We are going to meet on

_____.

Or maybe you are going to do this study solo, and that's OK too! God is ready to meet you and give you a powerful encounter with Him through His Word.

Each day there are helpful questions for you to discuss with someone else or reflect on personally. The in-depth Bible teachings will help you unpack Ruth's story.

The most important part of your weekly study will be your Q.U.I.T. strategy time. This is the place where you let God speak to you through His Word but also where you are open and honest about the daily struggles you face.

It will also help you evaluate what things need to shift in your life so that you can successfully apply the five habits from the Book of Ruth to every place you want to quit before it's too late!

And guess what else?

By the time you complete this study, you will have read the entire Book of Ruth and studied more than twenty-five Bible verses to help you persevere! That's a pretty awesome accomplishment.

Share what you're learning on social media with *#5HabitsStudy*!

HERE ARE SOME TIPS ON HOW THIS STUDY WILL WORK:

QUIT QUITTING VERSE OF THE DAY

These are the verses you will want to keep close by for those times you need to experience the power of God through His written Word. Each day you'll have the chance to study and learn how to apply them to your life.

SHORT READINGS

I'll be sharing a lot of my personal journey and we'll connect with Ruth on a deeper level through these sections. I haven't held anything back from you—the good, the bad, and the ugly parts of my journey are written into this study. You'll also read a portion of Ruth's story each week and look up other verses that relate to what we are studying.

My goal is to get you as familiar with the Book of Ruth as possible but also introduce you to other parts of Scripture as it relates to not giving up.

OUR Q.U.I.T. STRATEGY

This might be my favorite part! To overcome any battle, there has to be a strategy. This is ours! At the end of the week you'll have the opportunity to work through this strategy. Here's what the Q.U.I.T. strategy entails:

Q: QUESTIONS WE NEED TO ASK AND ANSWER.

It's so important on this journey to allow ourselves to wrestle with questions about the text we are studying, but also to personally evaluate the progress we are making. God's Word brings life and life-change, but it does require effort on our part. These questions will help bring you to this place of life-change.

U: UNDERSTANDING THE WORD

Here we will recap what verses, words, or characters you studied during the week. We'll make sure you have a clear picture of what has happened in Ruth's story before you move on to the next week.

I: INTO THE PROMISE

Every story in Scripture has a promise for our lives, and Ruth's story is filled with promises of hope. During this portion we'll see how we can step into the promises God has for us.

T: TURN SOMETHING AROUND

After filling up with truth throughout the week, here is where we'll decide what actions we need to take and what changes in our attitudes we need to create.

Are you ready to begin? Me too! Let's do this.

Week One

Becoming

THE

WOMAN WHO
DOESN'T QUIT

Most of the important things in the world have been accomplished by people who have kept on trying when there seemed to be no hope at all.[1]

DALE CARNEGIE

WHAT TO READ THIS WEEK: RUTH 1:1-18

WARM THINGS UP

Ask everyone in your group to answer these questions. This will help you guys start to build the much needed community for this study!

What made you decide to be part of this study?

What are some hopes/expectations you have for this study?

Where do you like to do your Bible study?

If money and time were no object, what is one thing you would want to accomplish?

What is something that tends to distract and detour you away from doing Bible study?

WATCH

To hear more from Nicki, download the optional video bundle to view Week One at *www.lifeway.com/5HabitsStudy*.

CREATE CONVERSATION

What is one thing you have started and quit?

How would you describe the difference between quitting and finishing?

What is something or a season you "finished"?

How much accountability do you like to have in your life?

Have someone read 1 Peter 5:8. How has the enemy blinded our culture to quit the "things of God" without even realizing it?

End your time together by praying and having everyone finish this sentence:

I want to be a woman who completes my God assignments because ...

Video sessions available for purchase at *www.lifeway.com/5HabitsStudy*.

ONCE A QUITTER, ALWAYS A QUITTER?

QUIT QUITTING VERSE

And not only that, but we also rejoice in our afflictions, because we know that affliction produces endurance, endurance produces proven character, and proven character produces hope.

ROMANS 5:3-4

Hi, I'm Nicki. And I was four the first time I quit.

My mom had signed me up for some soccer team my brother was on. It was one of those two-for-one deals, where she could have both kids at the same place and same time with a sibling discounted rate.

The problem was I had zero interest in soccer. Z-e-r-o. I wanted to be a cheerleader, the kind that flew through the air and did toe-touches like a pro. I didn't think the soccer shoes were cute. Running down the field was too much effort. And the boys on the team were just gross, always picking up worms and saying rude boy things.

So, I discovered a little manipulative move. It was called the stomachache.

You don't mess with girls when their stomachs ache, even if they are four years old. So, eventually my mom and the coach got tired of my soccer stomach woes and didn't make me finish out the season. They let me quit.

Wouldn't you know, one afternoon the coach knocked on our back door. My mom and I were so surprised to see him and wondered why he was stopping by.

It was to give me my trophy!

Me, the girl who quit, still got the shiny trophy.

Score.

I thought I discovered a secret that day: if you quit you still win. But you and I both know this is the furthest thing from the truth.

So began a lifetime of quitting for me. Some of the decisions I've made to quit have had little effect on my life. Other decisions to quit have left me feeling empty, broken, and hopeless.

I got tired of being this woman who sulked in defeat. I wanted to be a woman God would look at and say, "Yes, that's someone I can count on." For the past few years, I've wrestled with this question—why do I give up so easily?

That question led me to ask myself more questions:
Does it have something to do with my genetics?
Is something wrong with me?
Am I just lazy?

- What are a few reasons why people quit?

- Have you recently given up on something? Explain.

I haven't found a perfect prescription to this quitting problem, but I have found a way to persevere through the hard places, and I learned how to get behind someone who didn't give up. Her story is tucked away in the Bible—Ruth.

- What do you know about the story of Ruth?

- How much of the Old Testament have you studied?

I'll be honest, I'm not an Old Testament Bible scholar. In fact, I'm a woman who's just like most of you. I have a job, kids, carpools to drive, and a pug to chase down the street from the angry UPS man. (He's so over our dog.)

As we study this book of the Bible together, I can promise you may still have some questions left in your heart. There's so much we don't know about this story.

What we do know is this woman, Ruth, went from loyalty to royalty. God chose to bring the most powerful generational line in history through her—because she chose not to quit a commitment she made.

Through her journey I discovered five habits she consistently lived out. We'll unpack the first habit next week, but this week we need to build the foundation of Ruth's story.

There's a battle inside every woman that makes her want to give up on something or someone. With God's help, we can and will complete the commitments we have made. We, too, will become women who don't quit.

Let's take a closer look at today's Quit Quitting Verse: Romans 5:3-4.

> And not only that, but we also rejoice in our afflictions, because we know that affliction produces endurance, endurance produces proven character, and proven character produces hope.
> ROMANS 5:3-4

The first word I want us to focus on from these verses is: *affliction*.

- Circle all the words you would use to describe what affliction is:

grief	fear	sickness	hurt
pain	distress	suffering	tears
discouragement	peace	hope	sustain

According to *dictionary.com* the official definition of *affliction* is:

noun: a state of pain, distress, or grief; misery.[2]

- What is an area of your life where you have experienced affliction?

- How can going through an affliction make you want to quit something?

- What three things does Romans 5:3-4 tell us come after affliction?
  1.
  2.
  3.

Ruth's story is filled with affliction: loss, death, hunger, and uncertainty.

Through this story of affliction we will also see a story of endurance, proven character, and hope lived out in a powerful way.

These steps I keep taking each day toward becoming a woman God can count on have taught me character is the foundation for the assignments God has for each of our lives.

Sometimes I think we get so caught up in the pursuit of "purpose." What if our larger purpose is made up of small assignments and commitments that continually build our character?

I've yet to meet a woman who has a perfect character and can zoom through all of life's assignments with ease and comfort. Every woman I have ever met is someone who has experienced some type of affliction in her life. We are all in this process together.

While we may live in a day and age when kids get trophies for everything no matter what, there's more at stake than trophies in God's eyes. Eternity is at stake. Every decision we make to quit or to stick it out has eternal consequences.

So, the choice is ours.

Will we allow the afflictions of life to transform us or cause us to turn from God?

THEY GOT SUPER HUNGRY

QUIT QUITTING VERSE

... for if you live according to the flesh, you are going to die. But if by the Spirit you put to death the deeds of the body, you will live.
ROMANS 8:13

When was the last time you were hungry?

Like, really hungry? Could-kill-someone-hungry?

In the South, where I live, people don't mess around with their meals. We actually have a term for the emotions that hunger can bring: "Hangry."

It's when you are soooooo hungry you actually become angry. Being hangry is definitely a set-up for failure, quitting, and giving up. Not even having the right amount of food can make a person become angry like nothing else!

Right off the bat in Ruth's story we are dealing with a major hunger issue:

During the time of the judges, there was a famine in the land.
RUTH 1:1A

Famine. When food is scarce, people get all kinds of crazy. I think it's safe to assume there were some "hangry" people around.

We see the issue of famine pop up in other places in the Bible too, specifically during this "time of the judges."

- Read Judges 21:25. What does it say everyone was doing during this time?

- Why does it say they were doing this?

When I read the first part of this verse that said, "The period of the Judges," it sounded very official, organized, and like things should have been in order. Typically, when we think about the word *judge* in our modern society, we think about laws being upheld.

But this period was the exact opposite. Having no king brought a lot of disorder.

Imagine what it was like living in a world where everyone did what they thought was right in their own eyes.

Hot. Mess.

- Can you think of a period in your life when you did "whatever you wanted, whenever you wanted"? What happened to you?

Chaos. Disobedience. Regret. Those are the words I think of when I just start doing things my own way. The reality is, we will always have the choice to do things our way or to follow God.

I had to get to a place where I accepted the reality that each day I make decisions that lead me to follow my own ways.

A few examples:

- Listening to a sermon and thinking it's for someone else. My pride convinces me I don't need to listen to that Word, but God has something for me and I miss it.

- Coming to God with a personal agenda with my prayers. You know, those prayers we pray like, "God, here's where I'm struggling and here's what I want to see happen."

- Not listening to advice or wisdom from someone else because I think, *I have this figured out.*

When I make these decisions, I'm *feeding my flesh.* I'm not crazy about that word "flesh;" it just sounds gross. It honestly makes me think of Shark Week! Even though I don't use this word very often, the Bible uses *flesh* quite a bit so it's good for us to understand it a little more.

I dug around a little to see what *flesh* means in the original Greek language the New Testament was written in. As we study the Bible, sometimes we have to look way back at the origin of a word to understand how the writer really used it before we can understand how it applies to us today.

The Greek word for *flesh* is *sarks.*

Sarks is defined as *done apart from faith, decisions (actions) that originate from self or are empowered by self.*[3]

I have definitely made some decisions and taken some actions that had nothing to do with God's plans for me.

Our Quit Quitting Verse today is perfect for helping us understand what it's like to make decisions and take action without letting God's Spirit lead.

- Fill in the blanks for today's Quit Quitting Verse:

> ... for if you live according to the _____, you are
> going to _____. But if by the _____ you put to
> _____ the deeds of the body, you will _____.
> ROMANS 8:13

- Describe how you have lived according to your own ways.

Romans 8:13 offers us a solution for this self-focused mindset. It says we can live by the Spirit of God.

- How do we live by the Spirit of God?

While this might sound as complicated as my youngest daughter's elementary school carpool line, I think living by the Spirit can be summed up in two words:

Know God.

Know His character, know His promises, know His truth, and know the Word He has left for us to study.

Already in these first two days together, we have gotten to know God more. But let's keep going.

Ruth's story begins with a woman named Naomi and a man named Elimelech. They lived in a city called Bethlehem—the same Bethlehem in which Jesus would later be born.

- Naomi gave birth to two boys. What were the boys' names? [Read Ruth 1:2.]
  _____ and _____

Elimelech was a man who loved God, Jehovah, the one true living God. In fact, *Elimelech* means, "My God is King."

- Do you know what your name means? Take a minute and look it up on the Internet. Write down what you discover:

Things got extremely hard for Naomi and Elimelech in the city of Bethlehem. Food and work became scarce, which is so ironic because *Bethlehem* means "House of Bread."[4]

My husband and I have stayed rooted in the same area of North Carolina since we got married, but we have moved twelve times in fifteen years. Moving is my least favorite activity.

I hate the packing, the unpacking, the sorting through this, and tossing out that (and the struggle months later, *Why did I toss that out?!*).

Elimelech made the decision he was going to pack up his family and move to a place called Moab. He had heard there was food and work there.

A man left Bethlehem in Judah with his wife and two
sons to live in the land of Moab for a while.
RUTH 1:1B

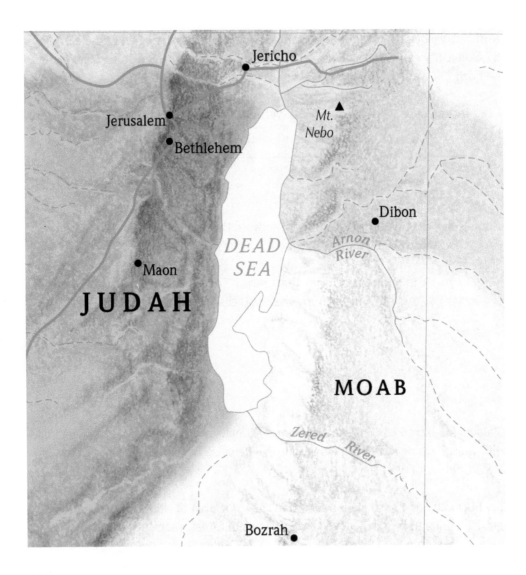

Some people believe that perhaps Elimelech was chasing a promise of prosperity in Moab.[5] Regardless of the reasons Elimelech picked up his family to move, one of the first things we can see from this story is that famine prompts movement.

When things are not working out in our favor, something has to change.

Typically, when we think about the word *famine,* it has a negative feeling, but what if we allowed those places in our lives that make us want to quit to get a little hungry, a little dry, a little … deathly?

I know I need movement in my life. Because for too long now the only thing that has moved me is the cycle of defeat.

The cycle of defeat keeps me in a place of continually being a woman who quits. I start something, it gets difficult, I start to feel hopeless, and so I quit. The cycle starts over just about every Monday for me.

To break this cycle, I need to starve those thoughts that say:

You can't do this.
It's too hard.
There's no way.
Your commitments don't matter that much.

- What are some thoughts you need to quit feeding today?

I also need to starve the actions that keep me in this cycle. Some of these for me include:

Failing to plan each day.
Not spending time in God's Word.
Isolating myself from others.

- What are some actions that would be on your cycle of defeat?

I've been feeding those thoughts that keep me in this place of wanting to quit, give up, and walk away. Romans 8:13 tells us we can be women who live by the Spirit of God, not by our own flesh.

Living by the Spirit isn't a stop-and-start cycle. It's a continuous movement. One which goes higher, lower, to the left, and to the right. It feels bumpy and awkward most days. And honestly, my thoughts and actions don't always reflect that of a woman who lives by the Spirit.

If we continue to live by whatever we feel like, we could entirely miss what God has for us. We have to get hungry for the right things.

- Read Galatians 5:22-23. What are the nine things living by the Spirit can give us a desire for more of in our lives:

1.

2.

3.

4.

5.

6.

7.

8.

9.

- Which of these do you need more of today? Why?

Learning to live by the Spirit doesn't mean the direction we are always supposed to take will be clear. But, when we stop feeding the places of disobedience and defeat in our lives, our steps will be firmer and firmer.

We're going to see that perhaps leaving the "House of Bread" wasn't the best decision for Elimelech to make. His actions weren't going to lead to the results he ultimately hoped for. Who hasn't made a decision they have later regretted? (Cue emoji girl with hand raised.)

- When have you been desperate and made a decision (by the flesh) you later regretted?

When I think about Elimelech picking up his family to head to Moab, he created a movement in their lives. But was it a movement led by the Spirit of God? We know he loved God, but did he trust God? Did he move too quickly?

It was a desperate time for them for sure. We can't say for sure if Elimelech was living by the flesh or by the Spirit. I don't know if Elimelech prayed and asked God for direction over this move. I don't know if he sought counsel from the wisest people in his community. And I don't know what Naomi thought about this move.

I've discovered the only way to recover from a bad decision is to make the next good decision. Let's starve the things that are keeping us in the cycle of defeat and let ourselves get hungry for the things which last.

TEMPORARY TEMPTATIONS

QUIT QUITTING VERSE

Be serious! Be alert! Your adversary the devil is prowling around like a roaring lion, looking for anyone he can devour.
1 PETER 5:8

My husband and I are first generation farmers.

Maybe that sounds interesting and exciting, but what it really means is we have absolutely no idea what we are doing. And our farm is a fixer upper, so that also adds a whole other level of unknown territory most days.

We spend a lot of time on YouTube and on Google, searching for answers from people who actually know what they are doing.

Since I'm a woman who tends to run and give up, I'm often tempted out here on this farm to want to put this place up for sale and move. Like the day our septic system overflowed in our front yard. Or the time I had to go stand outside for an hour with a hair dryer to unfreeze the pipes in the well. And when I had to figure out how to become a pig midwife? Oh my mercy …

Yes, there are many days I drive by neighborhoods and remember what my "normal" life was and my exaggerated quitting thoughts win. But, really this idea to move, flee, and get out of here is just my temporary solution to the many problems we've encountered out here. We know God led us to this property, and we know this is going to be a lifetime process of learning the farm life.

When I see my girls and their friends riding the go-cart around our property or look at the barnyard filled with baby pigs, I stop and smile. I'm grateful my temporary solution (let's move!) didn't become my permanent answer to a problem.

- What is an area in your life where you often see nothing but problems?

- What are some of the temporary solutions you often toss around in your mind?

This move Elimelech decided to make was supposed to be a temporary solution, too.

Whenever we study a text, it is good to compare it with different versions of the Bible. Read this version of the text in the King James Version:

> And a certain man of Bethlehemjudah went to sojourn in the country of Moab, he, and his wife, and his two sons.
> RUTH 1:1B [KJV]

The word *sojourn* means *temporary stay.*

See, Elimelech never had intentions of Moab becoming a long-term or permanent home for him, Naomi, and their boys. It was to be a temporary solution to a problem they had, but Elimelech could have never known, guessed, or been able to imagine the permanent effects this decision would bring.

Moab was not a place filled with people who loved God. They worshiped a false god named Chemosh.

In tomorrow's study, we'll learn more about these people who lived in Moab called the Moabites, but you need to know, this wasn't the safest, most promising place for a man who loved God to bring his family.

Sometimes along our journeys I think each of us are tempted to "make stops" in which we never intend to become permanent in our lives. Yet somehow they do.

- We miss one week of church that turns into two, three, four, and five.

- We drink one soda (which we gave up months ago), and before we know it we are restocking the fridge with every flavor of bubbly goodness.

- One night on the couch away from our spouse turns into a week, then a move into the spare bedroom, and then a move out of the house completely.

- Describe something that was supposed to be temporary but became permanent in your life.

- On the timeline below, write some "temporary stops" you made for problems that turned into something permanent. Try to come up with at least three.

```
├───────────┼───────────┼───────────┼───────────┤
```

For me, when I was nineteen years old, I made a temporary stop on my purity.

And, one cold January morning I found myself standing in a bathroom holding a pregnancy test that read "positive." My life was permanently changed.

I've made countless other "temporary stops" that led to life change. Yes, our God is a God who redeems, which we will see later in this story, but this idea of not allowing temporary temptations to lead us astray is why today's Quit Quitting Verse is so important to me.

> Be serious! Be alert! Your adversary the devil is prowling
> around like a roaring lion, looking for anyone he can devour.
> 1 PETER 5:8

There is an enemy of our souls who is always looking to detour and distract us away from the permanent plans God has for our lives. He will do whatever he has to do to convince us these "little" stops don't matter, but if we can become aware and alert, then we will have the ability to reject his predictable tactics in the name of Jesus.

- What is an area you can see the enemy trying to create a "permanent stop" in your life?

Here's the thing—while we learned yesterday that following the Spirit of God can feel a little unpredictable, the plans of the enemy are *very* predictable.

His plans always include:
Condemning us.
Distracting us.
Convincing us to go against God's Word.
Discouraging us.

- What are the two points of action 1 Peter 5:8 gives us when it comes to these predictable plans?
  1.
  2.

To be serious and to be alert doesn't mean we are walking around this world with fear, paranoia, or with a spirit of doom and gloom. Yes, we have an enemy who has a plan, but we have a God who is with us and for us!

While I believe God wants us to be aware and alert of the enemy, I don't believe God wants us rejecting the devil more than we rejoice with Him.

One of the definitions of *devour* is *to consume*.[6]

So of course the enemy would love for us to be more focused on him than on God. I think this is how many "temporary stops" are made. We become consumed with fear, uncertainty, and jealousy, and it destroys us.

- How has the enemy tried to consume your life?

- Read Deuteronomy 11:13 and write out the two commands God gives in this verse:
  1.
  2.

These commands offer the devil nothing and bring us everything we need to push through.

- Now read Deuteronomy 11:14-15. What is the promise God gives us in these verses if we do those two things?

Elimelech was consumed with finding food, security, and hope for his family. Tomorrow, we will see how this brought him everything but what he left home in search for. It was a temporary stop, which led to a very permanent place.

I am so thankful for the Bible and the way it can show us prophetic things in our lives. The deep, historical roots of this story have so much to teach us today. Whatever the effects of these temporary stops in our lives, they don't mean it's too late, it's over, or we're finished.

This story will show us that God is a God who restores, rebuilds, and renews—all things.

2 WEDDINGS & 3 FUNERALS

QUIT QUITTING VERSE

The LORD is near the brokenhearted;
He saves those crushed in spirit.
PSALM 34:18

OK, so we are three verses into Ruth's story and things are about to get a little out of control.

Naomi's husband Elimelech died, and
she was left with her two sons.
RUTH 1:3

Well, what on earth just happened? Where we left off yesterday, Elimelech and Naomi were in Moab and getting settled. And then, boom. Just like that, the unknown author of Ruth leaves us completely stumped.

But, here's something that might comfort our wondering woes:

Whenever we study the Bible, it's important to know there's a story time and story setting time. This story isn't being told to people who are living in the time of the Judges. It's not a real-life Twitter feed of what's happening. This story was told many, many years later to a different audience in a way that mattered to them.

It would be similar to us re-telling a story from our childhood to our kids. Our kids might not understand or care about some of the details of the story. So we leave things out. This is why as we study the Bible we may still have many questions in our minds about details it seems the author left out.

Like what exactly happened to Elimelech?!

I need to know these details. It's kinda like when my girls come home from school. I'm so anxious to hear about their day, and all I get back is: It was fine, good, or OK.

How did Elimelech's death come about? That detail was apparently not something the author felt like he needed to share.

Have you ever wondered what people will say about you when you die? It was a beautiful spring day. Our Carolina blue skies were near perfection. The temperature was just right and a cool breeze brushed beside me as I walked into the church. The weather just didn't seem fitting for such a sad day. Moments that mattered were shared, tears of sorrow were cried, and a life well lived was honored.

As I left the church I wondered, *What will people say about me when I die?*

I pulled out my phone and saw a new and important email had come through. I quickly clicked it open and read it. There was a big project I had been working on, and I was waiting to hear if I was selected. This email confirmed—I wasn't chosen. The first thought that popped in my head was, *Well, you should have quit this a long time ago anyway.*

My thoughts continued to spiral downward as I left the church. I was convinced the only words people would ever speak at my funeral were ones of defeat:

Nicki, the woman who never finished anything.

Nicki, the woman who quit.

Nicki, the woman whose dream died with her.

It was as though my cycle of defeat had moved me to a new level—despair and death. I felt like one of my dreams died that day. When a woman feels despair and death, she feels as though hope is as far away as it possibly can be.

I wondered if Naomi felt this way the day she stood over her husband's grave. This painful moment filled with despair, reflecting on the life of a man she intimately knew.

What his clothes smelled like.

His favorite meal.

The things that made him laugh.

Prayers he prayed.

I imagine as she was looking into the future, it didn't seem like there was much to keep fighting for.

- When was the last time you were filled with despair?

The good thing is Naomi still has these two boys: Mahlon and Chilion.

- Looking back on the time you were filled with despair, what were the things you saw you still had?

Sometimes when we are walking through places of despair, it's hard to see what we still have. It seems like so much is gone and we just can't seem to find hope ahead. This is why I love how God gave us our Quit Quitting Verse today: Psalm 34:18.

- What does it mean to you for God to be close when you feel brokenhearted?

I feel like whoever wrote the Book of Ruth was a to-the-point person because we are only about to enter the fourth verse of this story and see another life-altering event.

- Read Ruth 1:4, what does it say happened next for Mahlon and Chilion?

See, at the beginning of the story, we saw that Elimelech was a man who loved God. He and Naomi were Israelites, meaning they worshiped the one true living God, Jehovah. We can probably assume Mahlon and Chilion were brought up in the same faith.

- What type of women does the text say Mahlon and Chilion married?

- So, we have _____ites married to _____ites.

The history between the Moabites and the Israelites goes much further back than just in our study of Ruth. This isn't the first or the last time we see an encounter between the two. The Moabites worshiped a god called, Chemosh. Chemosh was an evil god that led the Moabites to do all kinds of evil things.

- Read 2 Kings 3:26-27. What does it say the king of Moab sacrificed?

- What kinds of issues do you think could rise up in a marriage with two very different faiths merging together?

And then, suddenly, things go from bad to complicated to really bad.

> After they lived in Moab about 10 years, both Mahlon
> and Chilion also died, and Naomi was left without
> her two children and without her husband.
> RUTH 1:4B-5

In five verses, two weddings and three funerals.

Wow.

This book is intense and we are just getting started. Naomi, Ruth, and Orpah needed God to be near. For those of us wading through these days where we just don't know what to do, knowing that God is near is comforting.

We don't have to quit. We don't have to give up when He is near.

DESPERATE DEPARTURES

QUIT QUITTING VERSE

Let us hold tightly without wavering to the hope we affirm, for God can be trusted to keep his promise.
HEBREWS 10:23 [NLT]

Not too long ago I was at the airport waiting for my flight to begin boarding. I happened to be seated right next to the ticket counter, which is a great place to do some people watching (a.k.a. my favorite activity).

I cracked open a bottle of Coke Zero® and settled in for the finest thirty minutes of people watching there ever was. Flights were being delayed and canceled like crazy because of a tropical storm, and since there were only a few flights that were still heading out, it was bringing all kinds of crazy out.

A frazzled mom with a toddler and frustrated husband walked toward the ticket counter. She frantically explained the exhaustion of what it's like to travel with a toddler and experience canceled flights. This flight was their last opportunity to get home, and she was willing to do anything at this point. She begged, pleaded, and even shed a tear.

Then, a gentleman, maybe around forty, stood behind her and began shouting his reasons for needing to get on that last flight out. His wife was going to be so upset if he missed her birthday, and he'd been traveling for a week. He desperately pleaded his case and told the airline agent she would be saving his marriage if he got on that plane.

Wow. Such high esteems for the airline agents.

But then, this little elderly woman came walking up, pushed her way past all the passengers pleading their cases, and banged her hand on the counter. She said, "You listen to me, young lady, I am getting on that plane whether or not you give me a ticket. I want to go home!"

With wide eyes, the airline agent told the woman she would need to calm down and step to the side or she would have to call security. So the woman stepped to the side but continued to shout her demands.

I don't know how exactly an airline determines who gets to squeeze on the last flights out, but I'll tell you something—either that woman won the plane ticket lottery or that agent just didn't want to deal with her anymore.

She was handed the golden ticket and made her way onto the flight.

We all react differently to desperate situations. And what we are about to see is Naomi, Ruth, and Orpah were no different.

> [Naomi] and her daughters-in-law prepared to leave the land of Moab, because she had heard in Moab that the LORD had paid attention to His people's need by providing them food. She left the place where she had been living, accompanied by her two daughters-in-law, and traveled along the road leading back to the land of Judah.
> RUTH 1:6-7

OK, wait. Let's go back for a second

- Remember when we were trying to figure out the logic behind Elimelech's decision to move to Moab? What does verse 6 say Naomi heard?

There's certainly a hint that maybe they moved to Moab because they just didn't think God was going to come through. Now, it's too late, and Naomi hears of the faithfulness of God. She thinks of the only thing a desperate widowed woman can do—flee to what's familiar.

She begins her desperate departure from Moab to Bethlehem with these two young ladies.

- Read Ruth 1:8-9. After they have already begun their journey, what does Naomi say to the girls?

- Why do you think Naomi initially made this decision to send the girls back Moab? Check the answer that best fits your viewpoint, or write your own.
  □ The sight of these two girls reminded her too much of the pain she had from losing her husband and her sons.
  □ She was too afraid of being responsible for them.
  □ Naomi wanted to be alone in her grief.
  □ Other:

A few verses down we start to see Naomi process her decision with the girls. She says things like she's old, she can't have more sons, and even if she did, the girls would be too old for them.

But then, in verse 13, we see the real reason surface:

> No, my daughters, my life is much too bitter for you to
> share, because the LORD's hand has turned against me.
> RUTH 1:13B

She's mad at God. Really mad. She's shaking her fist just like that little elderly woman at the airline counter.

- Describe a time when you have been angry with God.

Naomi's anger, hurt, and disappointment is making her want to quit these two girls. Orpah is the first to make her decision.

> Again they wept loudly, and Orpah kissed her mother-in-law,
> RUTH 1:14A

She goes. Back to her family, back to Moab, back to her god, and we never hear about Orpah again. But Ruth …

... but Ruth clung to her.

RUTH 1:14B

When I read this part of the story, I immediately thought of our Quit Quitting Verse.

Let us hold tightly without wavering to the hope we
affirm, for God can be trusted to keep his promise.

HEBREWS 10:23 [NLT]

Hold tight.

That's what I see Ruth doing in this moment. I don't know the thought process behind Orpah's decision to flee to what was familiar, but there's something deeper happening in Ruth that I think even the author of this book realized when he wrote the word *clung*.

I believe Ruth is clinging to the one thing she knows she has left that represents the God she now loves.

Maybe this marriage for Ruth was more than a love story between a man and woman. Perhaps it brought a soul change.

- Who is someone who has helped you feel close to God?

Whatever the reason, Ruth is clinging.

As we wrap up this first week, it's time to do our Q.U.I.T. Strategy. Set aside just five minutes to work through this activity, which will help keep you on track toward becoming a woman who doesn't quit!

Q: QUESTIONS WE NEED TO ASK AND ANSWER

- Were you able to complete all five days of the study?
  ☐ yes
  ☐ no
- If no, what held you back?

- What is one question the author of Ruth has not answered for you?

U: UNDERSTANDING THE WORD

- List all the characters in this story we learned about this week:
  1.
  2.
  3.
  4.
  5.
  6.

- Where did Elimelech and Naomi move from and to?
  ☐ Egypt to Moab
  ☐ Bethlehem to Moab
  ☐ Moab to Bethlehem

- List at least four life-altering events that we saw happen this week.

I: INTO THE PROMISE

- You studied five Quit Quitting Verses this week. Which of these verses did you need the most this week? Write it out below and share how this can help you step into God's promises for your life.

T: TURN SOMETHING AROUND

- Which of these areas did you feel challenged by God this week?
  □ Moving too quickly when I don't see God working
  □ Leaving because things get hard
  □ The need to cling tighter to God

1. Dale Carnegie, as quoted by Ben Arment, *Dream Year* (New York, NY: Penguin, 2014), 112.
2. "Affliction," *dictionary.com* (online) [cited 28 January 2016]. Available from the Internet: *dictionary.reference.com*.
3. "Greek Lexicon :: G4561 (KJV)." Blue Letter Bible. Accessed 28 Jan, 2016. *https://www.blueletterbible.org/lang/lexicon/lexicon.cfm.*
4. "Ruth 1:1," *HCSB Study Bible* (Nashville, TN: Holman Bible Publishers, 2010), 433.
5. "Life Lessons: Do Your Surroundings Show Faith?," *Trending Christian News* (online), 9 August 2014 [cited 28 January 2016]. Available from the Internet: *http://trendingchristian.com/life-lessons-surroundings-show-faith-ruth-11/.*
6. "Devour," *Webster's Third New International Dictionary, Unabridged* (online) [cited 28 January 2016]. Available from the Internet: *http://unabridged.merriam-webster.com.*

habit one

She

accepts

— THE —

ASSIGNMENT

of REFINEMENT.

Never give up on something that you can't go a day without thinking about.[1]

WINSTON CHURCHILL

WHAT TO READ THIS WEEK: RUTH 1:19–2:12

WARM THINGS UP

Go around and have everyone in your group answer these questions.

What was the high and low point of your week so far?

What is something you bought and later had regrets about purchasing?

Name at least two things you do well in your life.

Have everyone to share something that stood out to them from last week's personal study time.

Which of the Quit Quitting Verses helped you through this week the most?

WATCH

To hear more from Nicki, download the optional video bundle to view Week Two at *www.lifeway.com/5HabitsStudy.*

CREATE CONVERSATION

How would you describe the word refinement?

What is a high and a low point of your life?

What are some ways we can protect ourselves from becoming bitter through assignments of refinement?

Who is someone you know who walked through an assignment of refinement well? What were some positive things you saw that person do during that assignment?

When you are discouraged, what are some things you do to gain the courage to keep following God?

As you wrap up this week, have everyone fill in this blank and close in prayer: "I'm so glad I didn't give up on _____."

Video sessions available for purchase
at *www.lifeway.com/5HabitsStudy.*

ASSIGNMENT ACCEPTED

QUIT QUITTING VERSE

For I consider that the sufferings of this present time are not worth comparing with the glory that is going to be revealed to us.

ROMANS 8:18

We were sitting in gray chairs next to white walls, listening to the hum of the air conditioning unit. My legs crossed. His arms folded.

The memories of twelve years of arguments flashed before my eyes. The pride, the anger, the selfishness, the cold silence. How does happily-ever-after end up like this? And when did we decide we couldn't ask for help?

I know how and when. It happened when we decided to stuff our feelings and put Band-Aids® over deep wounds because it seemed more visually appealing than an exposed injury.

Years had passed, and we kept going until neither of us could take it any longer.

We now sat in these gray chairs next to these white walls. Our last effort. The words I couldn't say all those years before spilled from my lips—"We just need help."

Help was offered, and I could finally breathe again, but it was almost too late.

My marriage is definitely an area I've struggled to not give up on, and that day in the counselor's office I had to make a decision—to stay or go. I chose to stay.

Staying meant work, hard work—work that wasn't able to be fixed in a one-hour session. It was going to be *an assignment of refinement*.

As we pick back up with our story of Ruth, she's about to make a similar decision.

Orpah has left the scene, and Ruth and Naomi are standing on a dirt road with tears streaming down their faces. Naomi has repeatedly told these girls to go home, but Ruth is still clinging.

And then begins one of *the* most dramatic monologues in all of Scripture:

> But Ruth replied:
> Do not persuade me to leave you
> or go back and not follow you.
> For wherever you go, I will go,
> and wherever you live, I will live;
> your people will be my people,
> and your God will be my God.
> Where you die, I will die,
> and there I will be buried.
> May Yahweh punish me,
> and do so severely,
> if anything but death separates you and me.
> RUTH 1:16-17

Ruth offers Naomi *six* vows. Whew. That girl is for real. She is not messing around with this commitment.

- Circle the six vows in these two verses.

- Why do you think Ruth offered Naomi so many vows?

And here it is, friends—the place we see the first habit of Ruth, the woman who didn't quit, lived out!

HABIT ONE: SHE ACCEPTS THE ASSIGNMENT OF REFINEMENT.

- Fill in the blanks for Ruth 1:18.
When _____ saw that _____ was _____ to go with her, she _____ trying to persuade her.

Finally, Naomi stops urging this poor girl to leave her, and Ruth is in full swing of what could be the most difficult assignment of her life.

If we were to look back at the origin of the word *refinement* we would see it was originally defined as: *tenderness, delicacy.*[2] This whole situation is *filled* with delicate emotions, situations, and now commitments.

> • What would be the opposite of an assignment of refinement?

The assignments of joy, peace, and love are easy assignments for us to accept, but the assignments that challenge and stretch us are usually the assignments that make us want to quit.

Even though our Quit Quitting Verse today, Romans 8:18, had not even been written yet, it was almost as if Ruth knew the meaning behind it. She decided that no matter what else hard, trying, or messy came her way from this relationship, she wanted to see what God had in store.

> • Write Romans 8:18 in your own words:

Naomi made it clear that this situation was going to be awful, yet Ruth gives her an undying commitment. We have Romans 8:18 that tells us if we will stick things out, no matter how hard, there's something good on the other side. Yet, we seem to give up on things all the time.

I don't know about you, but I think I'm going to need some more time to unpack what it really means to accept an assignment of refinement in my life, so I'll see you on the next page tomorrow.

STIRRIN' THINGS UP

QUIT QUITTING VERSE

For our light and momentary troubles are achieving for
us an eternal glory that far outweighs them all.
2 CORINTHIANS 4:17 [NIV]

A few years ago there was quite a stirring in the city of Charlotte, NC. We live just outside of Charlotte, but we are in the city all the time. The president had planned a visit to our city to meet with the mayor, and for weeks leading up to his arrival, I was amazed how an entire city could get in such a stir over one visit.

Fresh flowers were planted beside the roads, and the grass was neatly cut along the highway he would travel on. Roads were completely re-done, and there was not a spot of trash on the side of the road.

I don't know if I've ever seen our city look so put together!

When the president arrived, roads were closed, security was tight, and people were going nuts over his limo passing by their office buildings.

I don't think it was quite the same presidential-visit-vibe for Naomi and Ruth when they arrived back in Bethlehem, but it does say the entire city was "stirred" by their arrival.

So the two women went on until they came to Bethlehem. When
they arrived in Bethlehem, the whole town was stirred because
of them, and the women exclaimed, "Can this be Naomi?"
RUTH 1:19 [NIV]

- Why do you think the entire town was stirred by Naomi's return?

I don't know about you, but when I go through something difficult, I tend to resist all the attention on me. I'm not likely to post an updated Twitter status with all of my vulnerable emotions and character-flawed situations. I tend to post only the highlights of my life.

There could have been multiple reasons for so much attention to be on Naomi and Ruth. Maybe people were really happy to see her again. What if they were still in shock over Naomi and Elimelech's departure? Is this a hint that they didn't leave on the best terms? Perhaps the community had gotten word of this tragedy and was incredibly grateful to see Naomi again.

- How does going through an assignment of refinement make you want to withdraw from others?

- Who do you want beside you when you go through something difficult?

I'm not a super private person, but when I'm going through something messy, there are only a handful of people I let in.

- How do you think Ruth felt with all this attention on her?

This time period was well before any fast forms of communication (i.e., mail, email, social media), so whether or not the town knew all the details of what happened, they certainly had questions.

- What are some inappropriate questions people ask when someone goes through difficult times?

> For our light and momentary troubles are achieving for
> us an eternal glory that far outweighs them all.
> 2 CORINTHIANS 4:17 [NIV]

Sometimes I struggle when I read today's Quit Quitting Verse.

When we are going through something that feels hard or messy, it's incredibly difficult to view it as "momentary" or "light." It feels heavy, permanent, and like the aches will never go away. But this verse offers us a hope-filled perspective that we can focus on when going through an assignment of refinement.

- What does our Quit Quitting Verse say makes our "momentary troubles" worth it?

I've been through my share of assignments of refinement, some you'll read about throughout this study. Some are assignments I'll never share publicly, but maybe one on one. I've kind of adopted the theme: *If God gets glory, I'll share my part of the story.* It helps me to stop resisting these assignments so much.

I don't want to ever put off the perception that I've got this thing figured out and my life is just full of cute baby pigs and DIY projects around the Fixer Upper Farm. Something powerful happens when we allow others to see how God is shaping and developing us. We share the common thread of these words: "Me, too."

- How can allowing others to peek inside your assignments of refinement bring glory to God?

Someone shared with me when she first heard about the topic of this Bible study—quitting—she didn't think it was for her. She went on to say she didn't quit things and she was doing all she was supposed to do in this life.

I raised my eyebrows and thought, "Wow."

I so badly wanted to say, "You've done *everything* God has ever asked you to do? You've followed every prompting your spirit has ever had to give, serve, and love? I mean, that's an amazing accomplishment. One I'm pretty sure only Jesus fully accomplished."

Because I'm working on accepting my assignment of refinement, I kept my mouth quiet and my heart still. (wink)

Heaven help us if we start to think we've got a handle on this life and we suddenly don't need the refining power of God.

So here's my prayer for us as we wrap up today:

Lord, help us not to get to the place where we start to think we've got this thing all figured out because an assignment of refinement is a place where pride steps to the side. We know we never arrive at this place of being completely refined. So help us to share with others our "me, too" weaknesses so that together we can keep taking steps toward Your glory. Amen.

THE BITTER QUITTER

QUIT QUITTING VERSE

Get rid of all bitterness, rage, anger, harsh words, and
slander, as well as all types of evil behavior.
EPHESIANS 4:31 [NLT]

I sat sipping my fresh cup of coffee, listening to her story, and hearing what God was doing in her life. My friend was about to embark on a journey across the country to follow after a purpose she desired.

I was so excited for her as she shared with me the ways she had seen the faithfulness of God through this situation. I was really inspired, but something in me ached when she said these words:

"You know, Nicki, when you're following God, everything just falls into place."

I nodded my head slowly, took another sip of my coffee, and held back the tears.

I was following God too. I was chasing the purpose, the dream, the plans He had for my life.

But, it didn't feel like anything was falling into place. It felt like everything was falling apart. Every time I seemed to turn around there was another problem, another obstacle, another detour away from where I was trying to go. How do we follow God when it feels like everything is falling apart?

I think Ruth may have run into this issue more than once on her journey with Naomi because as Naomi and Ruth arrive in Bethlehem, there's a clue as to how this journey may have gone.

- Read Ruth 1:20. What does Naomi tell everyone to begin calling her? Why?

- Let's read Exodus 15:23 to get a better idea of why Naomi would say to call her this. Why does it say they could not drink the water in Marah?

Bitter.

Now, you guys, I have been mad at God and others before, but goodness gracious— you *know* you are mad when you change your name to *bitter*. That is a whole other level of bitterness.

- How does someone who is bitter treat others?

- What do you think the situation was like for Ruth to travel as a widow and a foreigner to Bethlehem with bitter Naomi?

It's possible there were days when she felt that following God wasn't looking too snazzy and upbeat. This assignment of refinement was getting harder for Ruth.

When we are following God and it feels like everything's falling apart, if left untreated, disappointment can easily develop into bitterness.

- In verse 20, who is Naomi blaming for her bitterness?
  □ Elimelech
  □ Ruth
  □ God

God did not give Naomi the name of bitterness; in fact, *Naomi* actually means *pleasant*.

- Can you think of an example of something in your life God has named a good name and over time it's been renamed something negative?

Perhaps it's something like a job—when it turns from an exciting opportunity into a dreadful obligation—or when family turns into the people we resent the most. Even church or Bible study can become just another thing on a to-do list.

Using the chart below, think through a few scenarios on how a disappointment in your life could turn to bitterness, or quitting.

	DISAPPOINTMENT	BITTERNESS	QUITTING
	ex: You didn't get the promotion you worked so hard for.	ex: You start to resent the person who did get the promotion.	ex: You are so hurt you leave the company all together.

Naomi allowed a huge disappointment to become a definition of bitterness over her life, but Ruth allowed a huge disappointment to become an assignment of refinement over her life.

Before you think I'm getting all high and mighty and telling us we should all just be like Ruth, full of hope, let's be honest for a second. If I were walking through this situation I would probably be more like Naomi than Ruth. Not letting bitterness slip into my disappointments has been a huge struggle for me personally. I have definitely become a bitter quitter more than once in my lifetime.

- Who do you think you would be more like, Naomi or Ruth? Why?

I've spent some time trying to understand our Quit Quitting Verse of the day:

> Get rid of all bitterness, rage, anger, harsh words, and slander, as well as all types of evil behavior.
> EPHESIANS 4:31 [NLT]

I like this version of Ephesians 4:31 because I understand what it means to "get rid" of some stuff.

- Do you take time to "get rid" of stuff in your life? Why or why not?

When you first start to get rid of things it can feel difficult and confusing. You start to second-guess yourself and wonder, *Will I ever need this again?*, but after a while, stuff just starts flying out of the house. *Don't need this; don't need that.*

- What are some situations (whether past or present) that have left you feeling bitter?

- Do you think there are some ways Naomi could have "gotten rid" of her bitterness? If so, what would they be?

- Is there a way she could have healed without becoming bitter?

There's the potential for each of us to become bitter quitters when facing disappointments, but there's also the potential for us to allow every difficult situation to shape and form some part of our character.

When we start to see the hard, messy places as assignments of refinement, something shifts in our souls. It's a perspective change.

It's allowing ourselves to ask the question: How can this situation make me, not break me?

This isn't about getting it "right" or "wrong." It's about letting the hard things make us strong. As we get rid of bitterness day by day, moment by moment, we will stack these defining days—the days we didn't quit—and one day look back and realize we, too, are wearing the title: *I finished strong.*

FIELD OF HOPE

QUIT QUITTING VERSE

We are hard pressed on every side, but not crushed; perplexed, but not in despair; persecuted, but not abandoned; struck down, but not destroyed.
2 CORINTHIANS 4:8-9 [NIV]

Do you ever struggle with knowing what your next step to take is? Maybe you make the decision you are going to stick your commitment out and now you are wondering how it's going to play out. I have discovered with steps of commitment also come steps of uncertainty.

It was no different for Ruth.

Ruth and Naomi arrive in Bethlehem. They get settled. I picture Ruth with this look on her face, asking the question, "Now what?" Naomi shrugs her shoulders.

It was a good time for Ruth to ask this question because they had arrived in Bethlehem at just the right time: the beginning of the barley harvest.

Barley is a type of wheat, and we see it mentioned several other times in the Bible.

- What does 1 Kings 4:28 say barley was used for?
  □ to feed the goats
  □ to feed the horses
  □ to feed the fish

- What does Numbers 5:15 say barley was used for?
  □ an offering
  □ a form of payment

- How many loaves of barley bread does John 6:9 say Jesus used to feed the five thousand?

There's so much significance for Naomi and Ruth to arrive at the beginning of this harvest. Throughout the New Testament we see Jesus using the concept of a seed and harvest time in His teaching, and the harvest always signifies a time of new life after a long dead winter.

Remember when we talked before about the difference between story time and story setting time? The author of Ruth knew this concept of arriving at the beginning of the barley harvest was a sign of better things to come, which might be why he included this detail in the story but left out other details.

Even though this teaching is more than two thousand years old, the concept of the beginning of the barley harvest is one for you and me today.

Discouragement loves to tell us the best days of our lives are behind us, but the expectancy of a season of harvest stirs in us a passion to believe that the best days are yet to come. When we are working through these seasons of refinement, it can be easy for us to become discouraged.

We can start to say things like:

I'll never change.
This situation will never be better.
It's never going to happen.

Maybe we need to take on a little Ruth-spirit today and start to look at these seasons of refinement with a fresh perspective.

- Read Ruth 2:1-2. Who does it say was Naomi's relative?

- What is the question Ruth asks Naomi?

Instead of sitting around eating Hershey's Kisses® and vegging out on Netflix, Ruth asks a very specific question: Can I get to work? It's like she knows if she doesn't start to put some movement in her life she's going to fall into the cycle of defeat. She's tired of the grieving process, of feeling hopeless, and she's made this commitment. Something has to change.

I'm thinking today of all the areas of refinement in my life I'm facing, and perhaps, I just need to get to work on them. I need to quit talking about them, quit analyzing them, quit waiting for the perfect moment to get started and just *get to work*.

I'm looking at my kitchen this morning. It's a mess, and I'm tired of it being a mess. I've got to get to work on it.

I'm looking at the scale. It's not going down in numbers. I'm tired of this struggle, so I've got to get to work.

I'm tired of my thought process always convincing me I'm a failure, defeated, and not good enough for anything. I've got to get to work on retraining my thoughts.

- What is an area of your life that feels messy today? How can you "get to work"?

- What is something in your life that needs your redirection? How can you shift your focus to that area today?

Today, whatever you need to "get to work on," right now is the best time to start.

> We are hard pressed on every side, but not crushed;
> perplexed, but not in despair; persecuted, but not
> abandoned; struck down, but not destroyed.
> 2 CORINTHIANS 4:8-9 [NIV]

- What are the four things our Quit Quitting Verses tell us we are NOT as we walk through difficult situations:
  1.

  2.

  3.

  4.

This is powerful for us to know as we continue to wade through assignments of refinement. It will be hard, but we don't have to quit!

- Read Ruth 2:3. What does Ruth do?

Ruth finds her field of hope. She gets to work. The struggle we have when facing an assignment of refinement is not to believe the lies of how much is lost, gone, or over. I think this is one of the places where people start to give up on God. Look around you today. A field of hope is nearby. Remember that you are *not* crushed, *not* in despair, *not* abandoned, and *not* destroyed (2 Cor. 4:8-9).

IT JUST SO HAPPENS

QUIT QUITTING VERSE

Consider it pure joy, my brothers and sisters, whenever you face trials of many kinds, because you know that the testing of your faith produces perseverance. Let perseverance finish its work so that you may be mature and complete, not lacking anything.

JAMES 1:2-4 [NIV]

Our Fixer Upper Farm is surrounded by about ninety acres of farming fields. The first summer we moved in I noticed they had planted corn in the fields. I had no idea what the process for corn really looked like, but I found out that it was fairly simple. Put the seed in the ground. Grow the corn. Harvest the corn.

The harvesting for the more than ninety acres of corn took about a day.

I was *so* excited this last summer when I realized they had planted wheat in the fields because here I was studying Ruth, and this wheat field she was in with Boaz and understanding what it was like for her to glean wheat.

The day the farmers began to harvest the wheat, I was pumped. I was their audience of one! Watching this process was the highlight of my day. I stood out there waving and watching them all day long.

I know they must have thought I was some crazy woman who had nothing better to do with her time than to watch some men on tractors. The wheat harvesting process fascinated me. First, a tractor came slowly through the fields to cut the wheat. This took a couple of days. Then, they brought in a machine to bale the wheat. This took another couple of days. Finally, a truck with a lifting machine came through to pick up the bales of hay. That process took almost an entire day too.

When they were finished I went out to the fields. I stood there for a moment and imagined what it must have been like for Ruth, uncertain of what was ahead for her, the hot sun beating down on her back, the constant bending over just to pick up leftovers—alone.

This field of refinement would soon become a greater assignment.

> She happened to be in the portion of land belonging
> to Boaz, who was from Elimelech's family.
> RUTH 2:3B

OK, y'all—this is one of my *favorite* parts of this story. I love those words: "She happened to be ..."

- Why was this a good thing for Ruth to find herself in Boaz's field?

When a woman decides she's going to accept an assignment of refinement, she's going to have some of these "just so happened" moments. They're the moments when God's guidance, favor, and direction sweep in and things start happening we could never plan, prepare for, or predict.

You and I both know it's no coincidence that Ruth has found herself in Boaz's field. She said yes to God. Yes to this hard situation. The steps leading to this point must have felt uncertain and unsteady, but we are finally seeing a glimpse of hope.

The pursuit of perseverance in God is powerful. Let's spend some time studying our Quit Quitting Verse today.

- Fill in the blanks for our Quit Quitting Verse:
    Consider it pure _____, my brothers and sisters, whenever
    you face _____ of many kinds, because you know that the
    _____ _____ _____ _____ produces perseverance.
    Let _____ finish its work so that you may be
    _____ and _____, not lacking anything.
    JAMES 1:2-4 [NIV]

- Describe some trials you have persevered through.

- Do you feel like you are in a trial right now? Explain.

- If you are in the midst of a trial, do you see a "field of hope" nearby? Where is it? Who is in it with you?

Most likely there aren't a lot of people hanging out with you in this field.

Assignments of refinement don't seem to be parties people like to RSVP for, but I want you to know I'm walking with you today. I'm walking through my own seasons of refinement, finding glimpses of hope here and there. We'll just stay behind Ruth and keep looking for what we can glean from her. Don't give up on this process yet—it's just starting to get good.

Our first habit of the woman who doesn't quit is:

HABIT ONE: SHE ACCEPTS THE ASSIGNMENT OF REFINEMENT.

Using our Q.U.I.T. Strategy, let's look back this week and see all the places where the assignment of refinement came into this story and our own.

Q: QUESTIONS WE NEED TO ASK AND ANSWER

- What are my assignments of refinement right now?

- How is God trying to improve my character?

- Are there any areas where I'm resisting this process?

U: UNDERSTANDING THE WORD

- Who was the new character we were introduced to this week?

- What harvest season was going on when Ruth and Naomi arrived in Bethlehem?

I: INTO THE PROMISE

- Which of the Quit Quitting Verses spoke to you the most this week, and why?

T: TURN SOMETHING AROUND

Think of an area in your life where you have resisted refinement. It could be with your health, your dreams, your job, or a relationship. Write down a few possible areas in which God could be taking you through a season of refinement.

1. Winston Churchill, as quoted on *Goodreads.com* (online) [cited 1 February 2016]. Available from the Internet: *http://www.goodreads.com/quotes/523604-never-give-up-on-something-that-you-can-t-go-a*.
2. "Refinement," *Online Etymology Dictionary* (online) [cited 1 February 2016]. Available from the Internet: *www.etymonline.com/index.php?term=refine*.

habit two

she

follows

—— THROUGH ——

DESPITE HOW
SHE FEELS.

Remember that guy who gave up? Neither does anyone else.

UNKNOWN

WHAT TO READ THIS WEEK: RUTH 2:4-13

VIDEO GUIDE | WEEK THREE

WARM THINGS UP

If you could take a vacation anywhere right now, where would you go?

What is one of the best vacations/trips you have ever had?

What was something that challenged you from last week's study?

On a scale from 1-10 [10 being the most likely], how likely are you to follow through with something when you don't feel well?

WATCH

To hear more from Nicki, download the optional video bundle to view Week Three at *www.lifeway.com/5HabitsStudy*.

CREATE CONVERSATION

Who is someone you always know you can count on?

Do you think others consider you a reliable person? Why or why not?

What is an area of your life that frustrates you that you cannot change right now?

What is an area of your life that frustrates you that you can change?

Discuss the ways you have seen God give you the strength to do things you didn't feel like doing.

Close by everyone sharing one word they would like the group to be praying over them this week.

Video sessions available for purchase at *www.lifeway.com/5HabitsStudy*.

FEELINGS SCHMEELINGS

QUIT QUITTING VERSE

But You, Lord, are a shield around me,
my glory, and the One who lifts up my head.
PSALM 3:3

Is it any wonder that I woke up this morning and the last thing in the world I felt like doing was writing today's lesson?

Pinterest offered me so many ideas on how I could spend my day. I got text invites to go out to lunch, and I think I even heard my laundry pile try to convince me that doing laundry would be much more fun today.

The laundry pile lies—oh how it lies!

My calendar says today is a writing day. I'm on a deadline, so I've got to make a decision: Do I follow through with my commitment or follow my feelings?

I am a woman who definitely struggles with following my feelings over my commitments. I don't think I'm the only one with this struggle.

Recently, I asked my Facebook friends to share with me if they woke up and felt like doing what they were committed to do. Most of them said they did not. The ones who did feel like doing what they were committed to do were doing something fun or that they enjoyed. It's often the mundane places of life that convince us that following through with our commitments isn't such a big deal.

Unfortunately, life is not 100 percent filled with moments of doing the things we love. Most of life is built around the mundane, day in and day out tasks, which is why we need Habit Two of the woman who doesn't quit:

HABIT TWO: SHE FOLLOWS THROUGH DESPITE HOW SHE FEELS.

- List some distractions that keep you from following through with a commitment.

OK, we saw last week how Ruth accepted her assignment of refinement. But surely she got to a place where she had some moments when she didn't *feel* like following through with her commitment.

- List some possible excuses that might have convinced her this commitment wasn't worth it.

> Later, when Boaz arrived from Bethlehem, he said
> to the harvesters, "The Lord be with you."
> "The Lord bless you," they replied.
> RUTH 2:4

It's interesting that Boaz greets his harvesters with this greeting, "The Lord be with you." Not a typical statement for the boss "checking in" on his employees, right?

- What does this greeting tell us about Boaz as a leader?

- Who is a boss or leader you have served with whose presence always made you feel special?

- Read Ruth 2:5. What is the question Boaz asks?

- What if you have a boss or leader who doesn't make you feel noticed, seen, or heard? How can that type of leadership make you not *feel* like following through with your commitment?

- How does today's Quit Quitting Verse describe God's presence and protection around us?

The origin of the word *shield* is *ganan*. It means *to cover, surround, and defend.*[1]

- Read the following verses and unpack this idea of God being a shield for you.

Psalm 3:3: God is our shield and the lifter of our _____.

Psalm 33:20: God is our _____ and shield.

Proverbs 30:5: God is a shield for those who take _____ in Him.

I think Ruth was very blessed to have this kind, gentle, godly man enter her life, but let's keep in mind it hasn't always been this way for Ruth. She's stayed faithful to a bitter, hurt, and disappointed woman who was in the position of leadership over her.

In our own journeys toward not quitting, there will be times we have to serve under someone who has the potential to drive us toward quitting. I've definitely been there.

There have been godly leaders I have served with who make me feel like I could do anything, and then there have been those leaders who make me feel "less than." I've had to learn how to serve faithfully under both types. We can't allow the way others treat us to determine our commitment level to God.

Our Quit Quitting Verse reminds us that our God is a God who defends us. He sees all that is happening: good and bad. My job is to keep showing up and keep being faithful, trusting that eventually God will let the right people see what they need to see.

A good question for us to ask ourselves when we are serving under people we don't really like is: How can they teach me who I don't want to become? Pay attention to the words, the tones, the body language they use. Then find those Boaz-type leaders and ask yourself a similar question: How can they teach me to become who I want to be? They also have words, tones, and body language we can glean from.

- Who are some leaders you are serving with right now?

- What are you gleaning (good or bad) from them?

No matter what type of leader you are serving under right now, God is watching over every step of the process. Trust Him to see your faithfulness, and in due time, He will lift you up.

BIG DOESN'T ALWAYS MEAN BETTER

QUIT QUITTING VERSE

**Do not despise these small beginnings, for the
LORD rejoices to see the work begin.**
ZECHARIAH 4:10 [NLT]

It seems like I don't always struggle with showing up and following through with the "big" commitments of life: going to work, writing this Bible study, being at my three daughters' events, and speaking engagements. These are all things I have "shown up" and done whether I felt like it or not.

It's often the "little" places in life where my feelings start to take over. Like at 5 A.M. when I've committed to set my alarm and get up to spend time with God— I often feel tired, so hitting that snooze button doesn't seem like such a big deal. Or, if I've started a healthy eating plan but I'm craving chocolate, I often give into my feelings and eat what I want to eat. Not such a big deal, right?

However, what I've discovered about becoming a woman whom God and others can count on is it's often the littlest places that lead to the greatest destructions.

- What is a "little" commitment you often don't feel like doing?

- Why do you think it's easier for us to follow through with our "big" commitments" rather than the "small commitments"?

- List the three details the servant worker used to describe Ruth in verse 6:
  1.
  2.
  3.

- List three words someone would say to describe you:
  1.
  2.
  3.

- In verse 7, what is the question Ruth asked the harvest worker?

- Read Leviticus 19:9-10. What does it say about Ruth's right to glean?

Ruth didn't have to ask; it was her right. This practice was established earlier in the Israelites' history, but this shows us something else about her character.

Ruth just kept bending over and picking up what was in front of her—the big pieces of wheat and the little pieces of wheat. She didn't care what it looked like. Each step was a step of provision, and this became her process to reach the promise God would have for her. It was her small beginning that would one day lead to something huge.

She would learn to be faithful *here* so God could take her *there*. The Quit Quitting Verse today is a perfect reminder of this process in our lives.

- Fill in the blanks for the verse below putting your name at the beginning:

  _____ [your name] do not despise
  these _____ _____, for the LORD
  _____ to see the work _____ ...

  ZECHARIAH 4:10 [NLT]

- What is something you feel like is a "small beginning" for you?

- How can having the right perspective on following through with big and small things help you in your steps toward not quitting your assignments?

While you are out in the field by yourself, trust that God is putting the right things in front of you. Keep picking up what's out there—no matter how long it takes. There are blessings in the leftovers.

FAVOR PAST THE FEELINGS

QUIT QUITTING VERSE

Humble yourselves, therefore, under God's mighty
hand, that he may lift you up in due time.
1 PETER 5:6 [NIV]

My friend called me one day in tears. She had been through a trying situation and was ready to quit. What she was going through wasn't fair, it wasn't right, and there did need to be action taken, but the bottom line of this entire situation was my friend felt unseen and misunderstood.

As I listened to my friend share her struggles of wanting to quit because things weren't fair, I kept thinking about Ruth. Because Ruth accepted her assignment of refinement and she was able to follow through with her commitment despite her feelings, something powerful happened.

I think when we are going through an assignment of refinement our feelings scream all kinds of quitting quotes at us:
That commitment isn't worth it!
Those people make you feel awful about yourself anyway.
No matter how hard you try, it's still not going to work out!

▪ What is a quitting quote your feelings sometimes shout at you?

Feeling unseen can cause a whole bunch of emotional exaggerations to start, but let's take a look at what happened to Ruth—this woman didn't let her feelings convince her to quit, even when she might have thought no one was seeing what she was going through.

- Read Ruth 2:9-13. What does Boaz say he's been told about Ruth?

- How do you think knowing people had been saying kind things about her made Ruth feel?

- What instructions does Boaz give Ruth in verse 9?

> Then she said, "I have found favor in your eyes, my lord,
> for you have comforted me and spoken kindly to your
> servant, though I am not one of your servants."
> RUTH 2:13 [ESV]

And then, boom! She sees it. While Ruth had a dozen options of how she could have approached Boaz, she bowed low. She humbled herself and, in exchange, God used Boaz to lift her up.

It's like we are seeing firsthand, a real-life fulfillment of our Quit Quitting Verse today:

> Humble yourselves, therefore, under God's mighty
> hand, that he may lift you up in due time.
> 1 PETER 5:6 [NIV]

- Check the statement that best describes what it's like for you to humble yourself:
  □ Being willing to do whatever needs to be done to accomplish something.
  □ Thinking of others more highly than the way you think of yourself.
  □ Admitting your need for help.

People ask me all the time how I got involved at Proverbs 31 Ministries. While I did start off with a few volunteer writing assignments, there were many assignments that included taking out the trash, scrubbing the toilets, vacuuming the floors, answering the phones, and running credit cards through a machine—all as a volunteer.

It didn't always look like video shoots, devotion writing, speaking to women across the country, and helping lead thousands of women through our online Bible studies. There were many years of humble, quiet service.

There were times when I felt unnoticed. There were times where I felt like quitting. There were times when I wasn't sure if I fit. But, I was willing to do whatever needed to be done. I had no idea what God had in store for me through serving Him at Proverbs 31, but I knew I was called there—paycheck or no paycheck, speaker team or no speaker team, a writer with assignments or a writer with no assignments.

There are still many assignments I do without my name attached or without recognition. In fact, one of the things I love about our Proverbs 31 Ministries team is we have a trash rotation at the office. That's right—everyone on our local staff takes turns taking out the trash. Right now we are also in the midst of a prayer and fasting season. Every person on our team is taking a day to pray and fast for the ministry and for each other.

We know humility is a must for those who want to honor God with their lives. None of us wake up and say, "Goodness, I think I need to be humbled today," but it's the place where God is able to lift us up and take us to the places He has already ordained for us.

Favor follows those who follow through despite how they feel. Honor follows those who allow humility to shape them, and for those who do not give up, they *will* see the faithfulness of God.

- What opportunities do you have to demonstrate humility?

ASSUME NOT

Don't jump to conclusions—there may be a perfectly
good explanation for what you just saw.
PROVERBS 25:8 [MSG]

When you are trying to establish a farm, one of the greatest fears is that the people around you will sell their property to a builder. New construction has the potential to ruin the "farm vibe," and it can even force you into selling your own property.

Well, a few days ago a yellow rezoning sign popped up on the farm across the street from ours, and my heart got all in a tizzy. I started to think about all the scenarios that rezoning sign could mean.

Visions of a huge Walmart®, houses, and strange people walking up and down our long gravel road started to consume me. I started to think about what this would do to the traffic on our road and how much we would *really* be willing to sell the Fixer Upper Farm to a developer for. And what about all our dreams we had for this farm? We hadn't even started them.

I had us homeless, farmless, and broke in minutes.

When my husband got home that day I began to express my concerns about this rezoning sign. He told me he'd call the number on the sign to figure out what was happening. For the next few hours I was a mess. We had worked so hard on fixing up this property, and I couldn't bear the thought of losing it.

The next day my husband got home and casually told me he had called the number on the sign, and we had nothing to worry about. The farm was rezoning to become a commercialized farm, that's all.

I took the deepest sigh of relief, but then I began to feel a little foolish. My feelings often cause me to make assumptions that lead to the quitting road junction.

- What are some assumptions Ruth could have made about Boaz?

- What are some assumptions Boaz could have made about Ruth?

- What would Ruth have missed if her feelings had convinced her to see things in a light other than they were?

I don't always use *The Message* version of the Bible to study a text but I really liked the way it worded today's Quit Quitting Verse.

> Don't jump to conclusions—there may be a perfectly
> good explanation for what you just saw.
> PROVERBS 25:8 [MSG]

Because I am a naturally curious person and I love to understand the why behind everything, sometimes jumping to conclusions can lead me to frustrating places. However, I love this verse because it helps me remember to pause before I create more problems.

- How can jumping to a conclusion too quickly cause us to quit?

- Describe a time when you have jumped to a false conclusion only to discover there was a perfectly good explanation.

- Is believing the best about people and situations something you struggle with? Why or why not?

DAY FIVE

FIND REST

Come to Me, all of you who are weary and burdened, and I will give you rest.
MATTHEW 11:28

A few months ago I had lunch with a friend of mine. We were exchanging some ideas about ministry, writing, speaking, and leadership. Mid-conversation she looked at me and said, "Nicki, how do you do it all?"

Immediately, I felt sick to my stomach—did she really think I was "doing it all"?

Just that morning I had to cut a giant blob of dried ketchup out of one of my daughter's hair. Another daughter had gone to school with a pair of dirty socks on. (Where on earth do all the socks go?) No one's beds had been made. Dinner was going to be something from a drive-thru, and I had reached an all-time low a few days prior when I *forgot* to pick up my girls from school.

Seriously. I am *that* mom. The mom on the teacher's list to send multiple reminders about projects. The mom who forgets to send her kids lunches. The mom who needs ... grace.

I don't do it all.

I can't do it all.

I've accepted "all" is not going to be done.

So I looked at my friend and said, "I don't do it all, but I'm doing my best." She suddenly had a sense of relief on her face. Maybe today you are a woman who needs to hear this:

You are doing better than you think you are.

I know sites like Pinterest make us think that everyone's house is spotless and beautiful. Mommy blogs may make us feel like we aren't doing enough creative projects with our kids, and social media leaves us in the state of constant comparison.

My kids misbehave. We don't eat perfect meals. My husband and I argue. My house is totally clean for approximately one hour a week.

Quitting follows a woman who feels she can't compete with a to-do list that can never seem to be complete.

I will never be able to do it all but I have discovered a secret to living out this second habit:

WHEN WE GIVE GOD OUR SOUL'S BEST, HE GIVES US A SPIRIT OF REST.

Feeling tired or like we can't keep up with the rest of the world often leads to the greatest temptations to give up on something or someone. Even Ruth knew when it was time to take a break (Ruth 2:7,14).

- How can making sure you have the right amount of breaks/rest help you stick out your commitment?

- What is the difference between taking a break and quitting?

If we gave ourselves permission to get to an emotionally healthy place before making any decisions to quit, I think we would be a lot wiser with our process. People who stick out commitments are people who know their breaking point.

- Write out today's Quit Quitting Verse, Matthew 11:28:

- What are some things in your life that are making you feel weary or burdened?

Matthew 11:28 is referring to the things of this life that make our souls feel heavy, but I believe both big and small assignments can do this. To become a woman who doesn't quit, it's important for us to get into a rhythm of being able to lay our burdens down and take a break when we need to.

Of course, the presence of God is the best place to go when we feel tired or weary, but I also think our lives are filled with opportunities to refuel and gain the passion not to give up.

- Rate your success with allowing yourself enough breaks/rest:

|——|

doing really well   need some work   rest? never.

- Describe "activities" that bring you rest. For example: a long day on the beach reading a book, a hike through the woods, a quiet day at home in my PJs.

- Describe a time when you quit something because you just got too tired to finish.

Great job this week! You did it. You made it through our second habit, and you are on your way to becoming a woman who is stronger, more determined, and able to complete every assignment—big or small—God gives you. I'm proud of you! Keep going.

Q.U.I.T. STRATEGY

Q: QUESTIONS WE NEED TO ASK

- When have your feelings convinced you to quit?

- What burden(s) do you feel like you truly cannot give to God?

U: UNDERSTANDING THE WORD

- Write a summary of Ruth's story so far. What part of her story have you enjoyed the most?

I: INTO THE PROMISE

- Which of the Quit Quitting Verses has spoken to you the most this week? Why?

T: TURN SOMETHING AROUND

- Do you tend to pay attention more to the commands of your brain or the feelings of your heart? Finding a balance for both is important. Write down one practical step you can take in order to keep both in check.

1.“Hebrew Lexicon :: H1598 (KJV).” *Blue Letter Bible* (online) [cited 1 February 2016]. Available from the Internet: *http://www.blueletterbible.org*.

habit three

She

stays

—— OPEN ——

to the MOVEMENT

OF GOD.

——

Whatever course you decide upon, there is always someone to tell you that you are wrong. There are always difficulties arising which tempt you to believe that your critics are right. To map out a course of action and follow it to an end requires courage.[1]

RALPH WALDO EMERSON

WHAT TO READ THIS WEEK: RUTH 2:15-23

VIDEO GUIDE | WEEK FOUR

WARM THINGS UP

Play a little round of "Would You Rather." Here are a few sample questions:

Would you rather go to the beach or the mountains?

Would you rather live in the city or the country?

Would you rather eat Mexican or Italian food?

What is an unexpected gift you have received that you'll never forget?

Share something you discovered in last week's personal study time.

Are you a planner or do you like just to go where the wind blows each day?

WATCH

To hear more from Nicki, download the optional video bundle to view Week Four at *www.lifeway.com/5HabitsStudy*.

CREATE CONVERSATION

Give an example of a time you weren't sure what God was doing but ultimately experienced His faithfulness through the situation.

Is it difficult for you not to compare your relationship with God to others? Why or why not?

What are some things that have distracted you from experiencing the movement of God in your life?

Who is someone who helps you see a different perspective in your situation?

Video sessions available for purchase at *www.lifeway.com/5HabitsStudy*.

WHEN HE'S CLOSE

QUIT QUITTING VERSE

Draw near to God, and He will draw near to you.
JAMES 4:8

It's 3:38 A.M.

I stare at the clock and something inside me whispers, "You should get up." I toss, turn, and wrestle with my sleep-deprived thoughts for a few minutes before I finally climb out of bed.

Downstairs, I turn on the coffee pot and sit down in the white chair. Opening my journal, these words pour out of my parched soul: "God, I miss You."

Life has been moving at a warp speed lately. Work has been busy for both my husband and me, our three girls' lives are full, and someone always needs something.

The truth is I would pay a lot of money for 28 hours in a day. But mostly, in this stretched season of life, I'm experiencing how "it" happens—how people move far from God.

It's not always intentional:

The kids are sick ... so church is missed.
Carpool has to start earlier the next morning ... leaving no time for quiet prayer.
Bodies need exercise ... reading the Bible gets pushed aside.
Meals must be prepared ... so worship becomes secondary.
Reports and projects have to be finished ... you get the idea.

The list goes on and on of what can keep us from the closeness of God. I understand these struggles all too well, and I'm finding there is a great danger in these stretched times of life.

We can miss being with God, but we also can miss the movement God is doing in our lives. Missing God—either way—is tragic and threatening to our souls that long to thrive with God.

The third habit we see lived out in the life of Ruth, the woman who didn't quit, is:

HABIT THREE: SHE STAYS OPEN TO THE MOVEMENT OF GOD.

- What does staying open to the movement of God look like in your life?

For me, it's meant learning to live a life of surrender and humility. I have plans, I have dreams, and I have hopes. While I've seen the faithfulness of God through an abundance of circumstances in my life, there are still many things I'm in a holding pattern on.

There are people I need to see healed from disease.
There are places my heart longs to go and serve God.
There are things I don't know how to work out just yet.

When we can't see God at work doubting His existence and His promises become much easier, but when a woman decides she's going to stay open to His movement—even when she can't see what He's doing—something powerful happens.

- We've already seen Ruth display this in several ways. Can you think of a few ways Ruth has lived out surrender and humility?

Here are a few ways I saw Ruth staying open to God's movement:

- She made the commitment to stay with Naomi even though she had no glimpse of a hopeful future with her.

- Moving to a strange city, with new people, and a bitter mother-in-law, she didn't seem to express a fear of the unknown.

- Ruth got to work in the field, which just so happens to be the right one even though she doesn't know a soul out there.

I get what it's like to want to control the outcome of life, and to a certain degree, there are many things we can control.

- List three things you can control in your life right now:
  1.
  2.
  3.

A few things I am in control of is my reactions, my decisions, and my movements.

- Read Ruth 2:15-19. What does Naomi ask Ruth in verse 19?

We see that Naomi also had nothing to do with this field Ruth ended up in. It's not like Naomi hopped on *farmersonly.com,* saw Boaz was the most eligible bachelor in town, and convinced Ruth to get out in his field.

Learning to stay open to the movement of God is hard. It requires a deeper sense of trust and belief in Him than I think we may naturally have, but the Quit Quitting Verse today, James 4:8, offers us a powerful promise for this process.

- Fill in the blanks:

Draw _____ to _____, and He will
_____ _____ to _____.
JAMES 4:8

- What are some clues we've seen in Ruth's story so far that she was a woman who had drawn near to God?

- How close to God do you feel right now? Check the response that best fits you.
  - ☐ Super close. I've never felt more connected to Him.
  - ☐ Pretty far away. I've had times in my life I've felt closer to Him.
  - ☐ Somewhere in the middle. I feel close to Him but I'd like to feel closer.

To stay open to God's movement, we have to know what His movement feels like, and if I've learned anything about God's movement over my life, it's that the movement of God is one of constant change but consistent pattern.

Throughout the Bible, we see a consistent pattern of the unveiling of the character of God.

- Read the following verses and write out which characteristic of God they reveal:
  Psalm 23:6
  When we dwell in His house _____ and _____ will follow us.

  Psalm 34:8
  He is a _____ God.

  Proverbs 15:3
  His eyes are _____.

  Romans 11:33
  He is filled with _____ and _____.

When God is close to us, His character is consistently built within us. Learning to stay open to His movement is one of the hardest lessons we will ever become students of, but when we do, we will become closer to Him, filled with His character, and able to fulfill the assignments He has given us.

WHEN YOU DON'T KNOW WHAT GOD IS DOING

QUIT QUITTING VERSE

See, I am doing a new thing! Now it springs up;
do you not perceive it? I am making a way in the
wilderness and streams in the wasteland.
ISAIAH 43:19 [NIV]

Do you have a place you go when you feel like your life is falling apart?

I do. On the Fixer Upper Farm, there is this old, giant, majestic oak tree. I love this tree because it reminds me of the deep roots that are all over this farm. It's also special to me because it was one of the first things I saw when we came to look at the Fixer Upper Farm.

I'm sure it has a thousand stories to tell and many people have walked under its branches, but it's my special place.

Sometimes I go and stand under the giant tree when I feel like life is just falling to pieces—those days when we just don't know what God is doing, when staying open to His movement feels foolish and impossible.

- Where do you go when it feels like life is falling apart?

The day my mom called and told me her cancer had potentially come back for the third time, I went and stood under that oak tree. When my husband came home one day and told me his business was falling apart, I went under that old oak tree.

Under the oak tree, I pray. I wrestle with God. I often ask Him to help me understand how I could be open to what He wants to do through these situations. The deep roots stretch far under the tree and remind me that the promises of God are not just wishes or hopes—they are deep historical roots of our faith. If God did it before, He can do it again.

God can change our hearts in an instant, but sometimes it's a process.

I was so surprised when I saw Naomi's reaction toward this situation with Boaz. It's like something had changed in her. It's almost like she was able to see God's movement through Ruth's ability to stay open to what He was doing.

- What is the first thing Naomi says to Ruth in Ruth 2:20?
  □ The Lord bless him!
  □ That's awesome.
  □ I can't even believe this!

For a woman who was so angry, bitter, and shaking her fist at God to be tossing out statements like this shows us that *something* has changed in Naomi. This part of Naomi's story excites me because it reminds me no matter where we start, we don't have to end up there.

At any moment of any given day, we have the power to say: This is changing *now*.

We don't know how long this took Naomi or what her process to this point looked like exactly—but we know she got here!

I think one of the worst things we can do for ourselves in this process of becoming women who complete our God assignments is to stay stuck in the patterns that paralyze us. Change often seems to be a far off concept we can't always wrap our actions around.

Our Quit Quitting Verse today is from Isaiah.

> See, I am doing a new thing! Now it springs up;
> do you not perceive it? I am making a way in the
> wilderness and streams in the wasteland.
> ISAIAH 43:19 [NIV]

I love new projects, new opportunities, and meeting new people, but sometimes a "new" thing isn't always a good thing. New things can mean changes in our systems and processes that we don't necessarily like.

- What is something "new" that happened in your life you weren't crazy about?

In Isaiah 43:19 though, the Hebrew word for *new* is *chadash*, meaning *fresh*. Fresh is always a good thing. Who doesn't love a fresh start? Or a pair of clean, fresh sheets? And we all need fresh air!

To become a woman who is living out our third habit of staying open to the movement of God, we might need to accept a fresh, new start with God.

Even if you've been in the church your entire life—or you've been studying the Bible for years—I think there is a new thing God wants to do in each of us through this study. Will you be open to it?

- List all the areas in your life where you want to see God move.

- Now list an area in which you are struggling to see God working and moving through.

- What are some ways you are resisting the movement of God?

I want you to know that it's very normal to want to resist change with God. The older we get, the more set in our ways we become. Doubt has a great opportunity to settle into our hearts, and if we aren't aware of how closed off toward God we are, we might miss it.

But just like Naomi, none of us are hopeless.

HE'S NOT THINKING ABOUT IT

QUIT QUITTING VERSE

As far as the east is from the west,
so far has He removed
our transgressions from us.
PSALM 103:12

She had rehearsed her one line for days.

It was an important one too—the opening line. That morning she asked me a dozen questions about how she should smile, what she should do with her hair, and which of her shoes looked the most like pilgrim shoes.

She looked perfect and with script in hand we walked to the bus stop. Just before she climbed onto the yellow bus she said to me, "You'll be there, right, Mommy?" "Yes honey, I wouldn't miss it for anything," I said and smiled as she rode off to school.

At 1:00 P.M. I made my way to the elementary school for the much-anticipated second grade Thanksgiving performance. I took a seat in the front row and watched my little girl giggle with nervous excitement as she and her friends watched the parents arrive. They were so adorable with their handmade pilgrim and Native American costumes.

The play began with a song sung by all the kids. Then it was time for my Kennedy's big line—the one she practiced no less than 3 million times. The one she predicted would quickly send her to the Big Screen. And the one line I was there to hear.

She began strong, but about three words into the line my poor Kennedy caught a horrific case of the uncontrollable, inappropriate giggles. She flung her paper at her head and said, "Oh my gosh!" Her face turned fire engine red, and I could see the tears she was fighting back. There she stood for the rest of that fifteen-minute production with a paper over her face. She. Was. Mortified.

My momma heart sank as I watched my little girl fighting as she stood before this group her tears. As soon as the performance was over she ran to me and collapsed into my arms. With tears streaming down her face she whispered, "I messed up, Mommy, I messed up so bad. And I practiced so hard!" I tried my very best to console her but she wasn't having much to do with my, "It's OK!" pep talk.

Learning to stay open to the movement of God is sometimes a very humbling place. We won't always get it just right, and there will be times when we feel like a complete fool.

In the midst of accepting an assignment of refinement—following through despite how we feel and staying open to the movement of God—it can become incredibly easy for us to keep our eyes on ourselves. When we make a mistake, it's so easy for us to think it's over or it's ruined because we failed in some form.

- What is a mistake you have made that left you feeling defeated?

- What type of reaction do you typically have toward your mistakes? Check the answer that best describes you.
  □ I laugh them off.
  □ I try to cover them up.
  □ I become numb and feel awful.
  □ I have a good balance of letting my mistakes develop me but not ruin me.

I'm wondering how Naomi was feeling after her dramatic, angry-at-God entrance back into Bethlehem. We have seen her heart change drastically. And sometimes when our hearts take a sudden shift, we can be left feeling remorseful or bad about how we reacted toward God.

But one of the most powerful things about God is the grace He offers us through forgiveness.

Just like Kennedy's teacher had nothing but grace and love for her laugh snafu, God does the same for us—even those times, like Naomi, when we have shaken our fists at Him, thought the most horrible things about His movement, and flat out not trusted Him.

Today's Quit Quitting Verse is a powerful reminder of just how much God doesn't think about our mistakes once we lay them down to Him.

As far as the east is from the west,
so far has He removed
our transgressions from us.
PSALM 103:12

- According to this verse, how often is God thinking of the mistakes He's forgiven us for?
  □ All the time
  □ Sometimes
  □ Not at all

- How can not receiving the forgiveness of God halt the movement He has for us?

- Do you ever perceive God as any of the following:
  □ A judge?
  □ A puppet master?
  □ A police officer?
  □ A reporter just looking for a slip up?

I have viewed God in all these ways. And while God is a just God, a sovereign God, and a God whom we will ultimately have to stand before, He's not just sitting on the edge of His throne waiting for us to make our next mistake.

- Read Ruth 2:20. Circle the root word Naomi uses to describe God.

Happy	Nice	Kindness	Peaceful
Harsh	Mean	Strict	Rude

Wow. Y'all, this is HUGE for Naomi to be saying such a thing about God.

- Why do you think Naomi has had such a shift?

It's like she's free again. The bondage of bitterness is slowly leaving her and she's able to trust God again. She's living proof of what can happen when a woman accepts the grace of God in her life. She is able to stay open to His movement.

DAY FOUR

ALL THE EXCUSES

QUIT QUITTING VERSE

Pay careful attention, then, to how you walk—
not as unwise people but as wise.
EPHESIANS 5:15

I could write pages and pages of all the excuses I have made that led me to quitting commitments. But through this process of learning to stay open to the movement of God, I've identified the top two excuses that often leave me in a holding pattern with God's movement.

See if you can relate to either of these:

EXCUSE ONE: I DIDN'T KNOW!

When my middle daughter, HopeAnn, was about five years old she definitely understood the difference between right and wrong. Wrong was definitely when my husband and I asked her to do something and she just didn't do it.

She's a smart girl. So she started doing this thing when she was about to get in trouble for not doing something she was supposed to do. In the most high-pitched, whiny voice there is, she'd say, "I didn't know!" Kris and I would look at her and say, "Mmhm. You didn't know? We asked you to do this five times."

This phrase is a joke around our house now. Anytime someone doesn't do what they're supposed to do, we laugh and mimic HopeAnn's five-year-old voice, "I didn't know!"

But the excuse of staying oblivious has never turned out well for anyone. When it comes to the places we are having a hard time staying committed to, sifting through the excuse of "I didn't know!" is so important. Where is ignorance winning in our lives?

I've totally let the "I didn't know!" excuse ruin me. Sometimes it's been over something small. Like, if I'm on a healthy eating plan I don't always read the labels correctly: "I didn't know there were 3,500 calories in that. Whoops."

But then there are other times where it's something bigger. "I didn't know me not showing up for my volunteer role would leave you in such a bind."

- Describe a time when an excuse led you to quit because "you didn't know!"

EXCUSE TWO: THERE'S NOT ENOUGH TIME!

Of all the excuses, this is my number one. As I'm writing this, we are getting ready for back-to-school season. And I really feel some chest pains looking at our schedule and wondering how on earth we are going to make all this happen. I think we are going to have to sell one kid, at least. [wink]

When I first started writing, someone told me if they didn't have at least three hours to sit down and write it wasn't even worth the effort to try.

Well, kudos to them for having three uninterrupted hours to write.

That is not my reality. A lot of this study has been written in the carpool line or waiting for a kid to get out of practice. Thirty minutes here, forty-five minutes there—it starts to add up.

Don't believe the lie that you need oodles of hours every day to accomplish your dreams and follow through with your commitments. This is an excuse in the form of a lie.

- What is an area you often don't follow all the way through with because you don't feel like there's enough time?

I've seen what God can do through a woman when she decides to stay open to her seemingly small amount of time.

- Read Ephesians 3:20. What does it say God is able to do through His power in us?

Sure, you might have to make some adjustments [or sell some kids!] but if we look closely at our time and maximize the moments we have, we can do anything we set our minds to.

- What are the commitments you often don't feel like you have enough time to complete?

Overcoming this excuse has also made me deal with some tough personal issues. There are days when my exhausted head hits the pillow and I'm like, "What on earth did I do today?"

I feel like I'm busy. I'm certainly not sitting around all day with my feet propped up eating bon-bons and watching HGTV. I know I'm doing "stuff" but is that "stuff" leading me closer to my goals and dreams or is it just ... "stuff"?

Here is an honest question to evaluate when it comes to this excuse:

- What is stealing your time? Check anything you feel has been trying to take over your life.
  □ Social media
  □ The computer
  □ Kids' schedules
  □ Work demands
  □ Failing to plan
  □ Other: _____

- What are some of the excuses you find yourself using to keep letting these things steal your time?

Excuses have power and potential. They want to keep us comfortable, warm, and feeling fuzzy on the inside. Uncovering our excuses for this process isn't going to feel good, I guarantee that. But when you and I start to lay out all the excuses, something begins to shift in us.

It's as if we begin taking back our lives. Or, as today's Quit Quitting Verse, Ephesians 5:15, tells us paying attention to how we live our lives.

- Circle any area of your life you need to give a little more attention to:

Church	Family	Cleaning routines
Bible study	Budgets	Eating patterns
Exercise	Words you say	Thoughts
Processes	Work assignments	Relationships

- What are some of the excuses which often leave you wanting to quit these areas?

- Read Ruth 2:19-23. How has Ruth taken back her life?

- What are some excuses that could have left Ruth feeling paralyzed in this process?

- How is Ruth showing Naomi the way God has provided for them?

When we are in the midst of not being able to understand what God is doing in and through our situations, sometimes we have to ask other people what they see. Ruth has a different perspective on this situation, and her hopeful spirit is giving Naomi hope.

- Everyone knows someone who is struggling with negativity and the ability not to be able to see the blessings through the situation. Think of the person you know who fits this description. How are you seeing God move in his or her life right now? What are the blessings he or she can't seem to see?

SOMEDAY, ONE DAY

QUIT QUITTING VERSE

You don't even know what tomorrow will bring—
what your life will be! For you are like smoke that
appears for a little while, then vanishes.
JAMES 4:14

I loathe back-to-school shopping. Seriously.

I can think of a thousand other ways I'd rather drop $100 than on jumbo glue sticks, pink erasers, and Crayola® crayons. The buggies, the crying kids, and the 3,000 item supply lists make me almost break out in hives. But my girls get some very non-genetic rush from this experience.

"Oh! … Behold, new pencils! Ah … I've never seen THESE folders before! Mm … I just love the way new notebooks smell!," said their momma never.

While I do not relate to their school supply enthusiasm, their excitement gets me thinking about what our life is like during the school year.

Early chaotic mornings, after school practices, and crockpot dinners will soon make their return. I always tend to dread the routines, the schedules, and the busy days of fall. If I'm not careful, I will get caught up in life's seasons without pausing and reflecting with God about what's ahead. I feel like sometimes I miss the vision He has for me in each new season because I just get busy.

I'm convinced every season of life offers an opportunity to have a stronger response toward God's movement.

Most of us believe God wants to do great things in and through us but moving toward these things is often difficult. Thomas Edison said it best, "Vision without execution is hallucination."[2]

I don't want the plans for my life to be filled responses, like "someday, one day." Time is short and life tends to pass me by quickly, so I want to maximize each opportunity in each new season.

- What do you feel like God has given you a vision for?

- Do you believe you are in the right season of life to make those things happen? Why or why not?

- What might you need to put on hold for now?

I'm not a huge fan of putting any type of vision or goal on hold. I realize there are times and seasons for everything, but I believe this is another place we quit without even realizing it. The someday, one-day mentality often turns into never-day.

I think because I've struggled with being a quitter my entire life this is especially sensitive to me. God has given me this fresh perspective of what can happen when a woman sticks out her commitment from beginning to end.

And I'm afraid I'm going to miss it again.

- Do you ever worry you are going to miss what God has for you?

I once heard someone say every day we should do one thing to help us get closer to our vision. Even if it feels completely out of reach right now, even if we don't know what it looks like, we can still prepare ourselves to reach the promised place with God.

- Fill in the blanks for today's Quit Quitting Verse:

> You don't even know what _____ will bring—what
> your life _____ _____! For you are like _____ that
> _____ for a little _____, then _____.
>
> JAMES 4:14 [HCSB]

This isn't the most warm-fuzzy verse is it? But it's a powerful reminder of how short time is.

- What is something you want to be remembered for?

- If you were to die tomorrow, what is something that would still be left unaccomplished in your life?

Naomi is instinctively aware of this new season for Ruth. She also seems to be aware of Ruth's dreams and hopes for a better future. I sense a tone of urgency in her words to Ruth.

> Ruth's mother-in-law Naomi said to her, "My daughter, shouldn't
> I find security for you, so that you will be taken care of?
>
> RUTH 3:1

The word *security* here is rooted from the word *nuwach* which means *to rest*.[3] It's interesting Naomi doesn't say, "Ruth, I suppose you need a man." But what she sees Ruth needs is something so much more than that: rest.

Staying open to the movement of God is often filled with hard work—work that seems like we are going nowhere and not accomplishing much more than what we can see today. But when the time is right, the season is prepared and our efforts have been seen, God will bring us what we need.

Let's take a minute to recap where God has brought us so far. We've unpacked three habits now:

HABIT ONE: SHE ACCEPTS THE ASSIGNMENT OF REFINEMENT.

HABIT TWO: SHE FOLLOWS THROUGH DESPITE HOW SHE FEELS.

HABIT THREE: SHE STAYS OPEN TO THE MOVEMENT OF GOD.

We've seen Ruth accept her assignment, get to work in this field, something drastic has shifted with Naomi, and next week we are going to see some fruit from Ruth's no-quitting journey so far.

Q: QUESTIONS WE NEED TO ASK

- Why is it important in your own life to constantly remind yourself of what God has done for you?

- Which of the habits so far are you finding you need the most?

- How is God asking you to stay open to His movement right now?

U: UNDERSTANDING THE WORD

- How does the change in Naomi inspire you to keep trying and wait on God's movement in your life?

I: INTO THE PROMISE

- Which of the Quit Quitting Verses challenged you the most this week? Why?

T: TURN SOMETHING AROUND

This week we looked at all the excuses that could keep us from experiencing the fulfillment of following all the way through. Write down what a typical day looks like for you. Find a space in your day when you can set aside five minutes to rule out any excuse that could keep you from following through.

My Day

Get up   Go to bed

1. Ralph Waldo Emerson, as quoted by John C. Maxwell, *Put Your Dreams to the Test: 10 Questions that Will Help You See It and Seize It* (Nashville, TN: Thomas Nelson, 2011), 148.
2. Thomas Edison, as quoted by James M Kerr, *The Executive Checklist: A Guide for Setting Direction and Managing Change* (New York, NY: Palgrave Macmillan, 2014), 87.
3. "Hebrew Lexicon :: H5117 (KJV)." *Blue Letter Bible* (online) [cited 1 February 2016]. Available from the Internet: *http://www.blueletterbible.org*.

habit four

She

gives

—— OTHERS ——

WHAT
SHE NEEDS.

You just can't beat the person who won't give up.[1]

BABE RUTH

WHAT TO READ THIS WEEK: RUTH 3:2-18

WARM THINGS UP

If you could relive any moment from this week, what moment would it be? Would you do anything different?

Other than being a follower of Jesus, what would you want to be known for?

What is something that gets on your nerves?

Share something that stood out to you from last week's personal time of study.

WATCH

To hear more from Nicki, download the optional video bundle to view Week Five at *www.lifeway.com/5HabitsStudy*.

CREATE CONVERSATION

Who is someone you would describe as being emotionally generous? What is something you could share with the group that everyone could learn from him or her?

Finish this sentence: Right now in my life I emotionally need _____.

What is the kindest thing someone has ever done for you?

Read Proverbs 4:23. How will you need to guard your heart as you are learning to be emotionally generous?

End your time together in prayer and by having everyone look through the daily Quit Quitting Verses of the week. As a group, pick one verse you want to memorize together. Text this verse to each other, pray it over one another, and next week quote it to each other!

Video sessions available for purchase at *www.lifeway.com/5HabitsStudy*.

STOP RIGHT THERE

QUIT QUITTING VERSE

Give, and it will be given to you; a good measure—pressed down, shaken together, and running over—will be poured into your lap. For with the measure you use, it will be measured back to you.
LUKE 6:38

The bus stop for my girls is at the end of our long gravel road. Most days I am a mean momma and make them walk all the way there. But a few weeks ago I was on my way to work early so I decided I would drop them off.

We were sitting in the car when the bus pulled up. The bus's stop sign went out, and my girls began to cross the street. When out of nowhere, a car's brakes started screeching and into the soybean field the car went. The car was *inches* away from hitting both of my girls, and they stood in the street paralyzed with fear.

I started to get out of the car to confront the driver when he took off down our gravel road. I know he must have thought there was a way out, but it's a dead end down our road, which he was about to discover.

Something fierce came out in me as I realized he was trying to make a run for it. So there I stood in the middle of the road, hands on the hips and all. He turned his car around and slowly began to make his way toward me. Then he started to speed up, like he was going to try to go around me!

He was messing with the wrong momma, on the wrong day. So I stood in the middle of the road, with my hands on my hips and shouted to him to stop RIGHT THERE.

He rolled his window down and we began a rather unpleasant exchange of words. He tried to blame the car in front of him, saying that they slammed on the brakes at the last minute, but I had seen the entire thing. The car in front of him was completely stopped.

What I needed was for this man to give me an apology, but all he was doing was making excuses. I took a deep breath and realized I was about to have to live out the fourth habit of Ruth, the woman who didn't quit.

HABIT FOUR: SHE GIVES OTHERS WHAT SHE NEEDS.

I calmed myself down and I looked at him and said, "You almost killed someone today, but you didn't. This was a wake-up call for both of us. I hope you'll pay attention more carefully when you're driving on this road from now on." He shook his head in agreement and said, "I'm really sorry."

This fourth habit is wrapped in something called *emotional generosity*.

Emotional generosity is the hardest form of generosity there is to give. It's incredibly easy for me to write a check or donate an item, but what about not giving people what I think they deserve for how they've treated me?

It's a rough, sticky, messy, beautiful process.

We live in a world that teaches us to live by the "eye for an eye" mantra, so this habit goes against the grain of our culture for sure.

Where we are picking back up in Ruth's story this week isn't the first time we have seen emotional generosity lived out in her. But it is where we are going to see what is on the other side of a season of giving others what we need.

- At the beginning of the story, what were the things Ruth and Naomi needed the most? Circle everything they needed.

Safety   Security   Food   Shelter   Money

- Now circle what they needed emotionally.

Joy   Peace   Hope   Positivity

- How has Ruth offered those things to Naomi throughout the story so far?

- Did we see Naomi offer any of these things to Ruth?
  - ☐ As little as possible
  - ☐ Not at all
  - ☐ The entire way

While we haven't seen a whole lot of Nice Naomi, we have seen that something has shifted in her. For the first time in this story, we are about to see Naomi give Ruth what she truly needs—wise counsel.

> And now is not Boaz of our kindred, with whose maidens thou wast? Behold, he winnoweth barley to night in the threshing floor.
> RUTH 3:2 [KJV]

Let's be real for a second, this verse kind of sounds like something out of a Shakespearean play. What on earth is winnowing and what is a threshing floor? And why is Naomi bringing this up?

OK, let's break this down.

Here's how the Bible dictionary describes the process of winnowing: "A step in the processing of grain whereby the grain is separated from the inedible parts. The stalks are thrown into the air, and the wind blows away the chaff and the straw, letting the heavier pure grain fall back to the ground (Isa. 30:24)."[2]

The threshing floor is the place the barley was stored.

Here we are seeing another clue into Boaz's personality, especially when it comes to his business. He is all hands on deck. He's involved in the wheat harvesting process from the beginning to the end. Most likely he was there sleeping because he wanted to protect his barley from any robbers. I find it interesting though, that Boaz, the owner of this barely, hasn't hired someone else to protect his crop and winnow it.

Now we are still left with one question: Why is Naomi bringing this up?

- Read Ruth 3:3-4. Are you even more confused? We are going to look at the possibilities of what could be going on, but before we wrap this up today, write out today's Quit Quitting Verse:

- What is the kindest thing someone has ever done for you?

- Who is someone whom you did not expect to show you kindness?

- How do you feel about this concept of being emotionally generous?
  □ I'm excited to learn more.
  □ A little excited—this is going to be hard for me.
  □ I think this is the dumbest idea in the world.

- Circle all the emotional things you would like more of in your life.
  peace   joy   companionship   counsel   wisdom   empathy

This habit is going to take some time for us to develop a desire for. But the more you work through it, the more I promise you'll see how powerful this concept can be.

GET TO THE ROOT

Guard your heart above all else, for it is the source of life.
PROVERBS 4:23

For the past few days around 3:00 P.M. in the afternoon I have felt like I could literally fall asleep, anywhere, anytime. In fact, yesterday I did. I laid down on the couch just for a few minutes so I could get some energy back up and ended up asleep for thirty minutes!

This is very out of character and I started to get concerned something was wrong with me.

I prayed for this sense of exhaustion to leave me. I read Bible verses on strength, and I even changed my diet to make sure it wasn't something I was eating. When all that failed, I started drinking coffee in the afternoon—and that didn't help either. This morning, I sat down and thought through *everything* I had done this past week.

I started to wonder if something had changed with the allergy medicine I took every year. This certain brand of allergy medicine claims to be 24-hour-non-drowsy, but as I googled it I realized others had the same complaint. Something had changed with the ingredients, and many others were feeling the sluggish afternoon vibe too.

I stopped taking the medicine and instantly felt better.

As we continue to live out this fourth habit of giving others what we need, we have to get down to the root of the issues. I wish this process could be as easy as to stop taking a medicine to instantly feel better, but it's often not.

Here's what I've learned about roots:

They tend to run deep.

It will be almost impossible for us to learn to give others what we need if we don't work through the issues that keep us from being emotionally generous.

I'm seeing Naomi—who was able to work through her bitterness issues with God—at a place where she is finally able to give Ruth what she needs: instruction.

> Wash, put on perfumed oil, and wear your best clothes. Go down to the threshing floor, but don't let the man know you are there until he has finished eating and drinking. When he lies down, notice the place where he's lying, go in and uncover his feet, and lie down. Then he will explain to you what you should do.
> RUTH 3:3-4

- What three things does Naomi instruct Ruth to do to prepare herself to enter into this conversation with Boaz?
  1.
  2.
  3.

- Where does Naomi instruct Ruth to go?
  □ The field
  □ The threshing floor
  □ The celebration party

- How do you think Ruth felt about this?

Oh, the many thoughts Ruth must have been having at this moment. What would she wear? What was a smell Boaz liked? What would she say? What I love the most about this, is that Ruth was at a place in her soul where she was able to receive the instruction Naomi was offering her.

- How can you apply Ruth's teachable spirit to a situation you want to give up on?

- What is the instruction God gives us in our Quit Quitting Verse, Proverbs 4:23?

I find myself needing to guard my heart in the area of social media. It can be really easy to look at the highlights of everyone else's life and think my life is just plain sad, so I've allowed myself to post some more of the authentic moments in my life. You know, those Pinterest projects that don't turn out just right or other mishaps that happen along the way that I've learned to laugh at.

I do so in hopes that other women will see my life isn't perfect, I make mistakes, and things don't always turn out as I planned or desired.

- What are some areas of your life where you need to guard your heart?

In order to give others what we need, we have to know how to protect our hearts from the things we don't need. If looking at someone's feed on Facebook makes my heart unwell, I don't need that. I give myself permission to hide their account from my feed.

We have to do what we need to do to keep our soul well.

Then, we will be able to be at this place where we are finding Naomi—with the ability to give to others kindness, gentleness, wisdom, and peace.

- What specifically do you need to give yourself permission to do in order to guard your heart?

Ruth needs a husband; Naomi sees this need. They are both able to give and receive what they need because they have learned to guard their hearts. As we learn to guard our hearts from the things we *don't* need, we will be able to give others the things we *do* need.

LISTEN WELL

Listen, my son, and be wise.
PROVERBS 23:19 [NIV]

What if I don't have what it takes to give others what I need?

I see myself standing at the bottom of the giant mountain today. I feel small, unnoticed, not capable, and unworthy. And that question is haunting me.

My heart is filled with passion—yet here I sit … wondering, *Will I really be able to do this?*

Something inside me whispers, "You can do it, but it will be up to you if you do."

Then, I fail. Disobeying. Giving others what I think they deserve: a rude comment back, a cold shoulder, or an action that reflected what they just did to me. What am I doing wrong? I feel like I've always had a harder struggle than most people.

Even as a little girl, things were always hard for me. In fact, I had to complete Kindergarten twice. You can laugh; I have too.

It's always been harder for me to accomplish things. Not a learning disability type struggle, but I feel like I have a deeper struggle with weakness than most people.

My tennis coach in high school noticed it too, "Chevalier [my maiden name], you are just gonna have to work harder than any of these other girls if you want to win a match!" So I spent hours and hours on the tennis courts, only to win one match that entire season.

Nothing has ever seemed to come easily for me.

Some people seem just to be good at life naturally. They make small efforts that go a long way. Success seems to follow them wherever they go. I have people like this in my life; they are great people, too! I realize, each of us has our own struggles. But one of my greatest fears is because of my abundance of weakness: I will never accomplish my God-given dreams.

I'm always deeply struggling to keep up. Hours of writing. Hours of message prep. Hours of thinking. I spend more time preparing to do the things God has called me to do than actually DOING the things. And so the tasks that often lay before me make me feel like I can never be successful at anything.

Here's the problem: in order to be successful at all my God-struggles, I have the answers I need. Others have given me instruction, but I don't always want to follow it.

- My friend Lisa has given me instruction on how to better manage my time.

- Weight-loss books have given me instruction on how to lose weight.

- Workout instructors have given me instructions on how to workout.

- Writer workshops have given me instruction on ways to make my writing better.

We live in a world where most of the answers to our quitting struggles are at the tips of our fingers. But we have to be willing to follow instruction—from God and from others.

Yesterday, we saw how open to Naomi's instruction Ruth was. Now, we see Ruth's reaction.

> So Ruth said to her, "I will do everything you say."
> RUTH 3:5

- Are you surprised at Ruth's willingness to follow Naomi's instruction?
  □ Yes
  □ No
  □ A little

- On a scale of 1 to 10 (10 being the most open), put a dot on the line to show how open to following instruction you are right now?

| 1 | 2 | 3 | 4 | 5 | 6 | 7 | 8 | 9 | 10 |

Look up the following verses and write down the instruction God gives us when it comes to being emotionally generous with someone else.

THE VERSE	THE INSTRUCTION
Proverbs 24:17	
Luke 6:31	
Romans 12:18	
Ephesians 4:23	
1 John 3:16	

And these are just a few of the many verses that provide us with specific instructions on how to give others what we need. But will we listen?

- Write out today's Quit Quitting Verse: Proverbs 23:19.

Are you listening? Are you setting your heart on the right path to finish this journey strong? If this doesn't come easy for you, I totally get it. I'm right here with you, friend. Together, we'll just keep taking step by step to live out these habits.

- As we wrap up today, take two minutes and write out a prayer to God. Ask Him to show you what you are struggling to hear and follow through with.

_____

_____

_____

_____

_____

_____

_____

_____

_____

_____

_____

_____

_____

_____

_____

_____

_____

_____

_____

_____

DAY FOUR:

RISKING REJECTION

The second is: Love your neighbor as yourself. There
is no other command greater than these.
MARK 12:31

We hadn't seen each other in a few weeks and I was super excited to catch up on
my friend's life. Arriving at the restaurant, we hugged, took our seats, and ordered
some sweet tea. Immediately, we started talking about what had been going on in
our lives and dug into a discussion about the previous month's events.

Just a few minutes into our catch-up session, a person's name (whom I didn't care
for) came up. My friend told me a story that made me dislike this person even
more. I then told my friend a story about this same person that made her dislike
that person more, too. And so our conversation went.

When I left the restaurant, there was a sick feeling inside me. My thoughts wan-
dered through our conversation and I felt deeply convicted it'd been nothing but
idle talk.

The crazy thing was, in the midst of the conversation, I didn't even realize what
was happening. I thought I was just catching up with an old friend. The reality is,
I was gossiping.

I wish I could tell you this eye-opening moment changed me and I never spoke
badly of someone again. But I am a woman who consistently finds herself starting
over, trying again, and not giving up on this process.

The truth is: becoming emotionally generous is risky.

That day at lunch with my friend, if I would have said something about not talking
about that other person, there was a risk my friend may have thought I was judging
her or being a goody-two-shoes.

There's always the chance others might reject our emotional offerings. As we pick back up with our Ruth, she's also in a risky place of the potential emotional rejection from Boaz.

- Read Ruth 3:6-15. When Ruth laid at Boaz's feet, do you think it was a sign of:
  ☐ Desperation
  ☐ Obedience
  ☐ Submission

- In verse 9, how did Ruth respond to Boaz's question about who she was?

> Spread the corner of your garment over me, since
> you are a guardian-redeemer of our family.
> RUTH 3:9B [NIV]

For Ruth to say this was basically her inquiring of Boaz's willingness to take her in as his wife. Can you imagine how nervous she must have been while waiting to see Boaz's reaction toward her?

There are so many different ways Boaz could have reacted toward Ruth. He certainly could have asked her to leave but he didn't.

> The LORD bless you, my daughter," he replied. "This kindness is
> greater than that which you showed earlier: You have not run after
> the younger men, whether rich or poor. And now, my daughter,
> don't be afraid. I will do for you all you ask. All the people of
> my town know that you are a woman of noble character.
> RUTH 3:10-11 [NIV]

- What are the things about Ruth's character Boaz mentioned?

- How do you think Ruth reacted toward his response?
  - □ Excited: She screamed like a schoolgirl.
  - □ Shy: Her face turned fire-engine red.
  - □ Relieved: She took the deepest sigh of relief.

Those are all emotionally generous things Ruth needed to hear. I think this is a beautiful reminder for us to hold onto the next time we are afraid of someone's emotional reaction toward us.

- Who is someone you are afraid of being emotionally generous toward because there is a fear of them rejecting you?

- What do you need most from that person? Acceptance? Love? Forgiveness?

- Today's Quit Quitting Verse, Mark 12:31, tells us what the second greatest command is. Read Mark 12:30, what does it say is the greatest command?

- How can learning to love God with your heart and soul help you love yourself well?

- How does loving yourself well help you love others well?

We will always have the risk of rejection in all our relationships except in one: the relationship we have with God. Just like Boaz greeted Ruth with love, honor, and respect, God greets us the same way.

Sometimes I have this fear that God might reject me because I keep messing up, I keep quitting, and I keep getting far from His commands. But God is the creator of emotional generosity.

No matter where you find yourself with Him today, He's present, greeting you with the kindest, most surprising words.

FROM DISTRACTED TO DETERMINED

QUIT QUITTING VERSE

We do this by keeping our eyes on Jesus, the
champion who initiates and perfects our faith.
HEBREWS 12:2 [NLT]

I have this love/hate relationship with the Internet. Most days I think it's totally
awesome but those are not the days when I have deadlines and "real work" that
has to get done. It's so tempting when you are sitting at your computer working not
to get distracted and detoured away by social media, a pretty picture, or a funny
YouTube video.

I'm just going to be honest—some days, the Internet wins. It convinces me that
productivity has everything to do with clicking this or clicking that.

The Internet isn't the only place that will try to distract us. As we wrap up this
fourth habit—she gives others what she needs—I can promise there will be some
distractions along the way.

- What are some distractions you are facing right now, even as you
  try to complete this Bible study?

Distractions can easily become defeat if we don't keep them in check.

Ruth is about to encounter a *big* distraction in this situation with Boaz.

Yes, it is true that I am a family redeemer, but there is
a redeemer closer than I am. Stay here tonight, and in
the morning, if he wants to redeem you, that's good. Let
him redeem you. But if he doesn't want to redeem you,
as the Lord lives, I will. Now lie down until morning.

RUTH 3:12-13

What? There's another man in line. Oh, mercy.

Doesn't it always seem like just as things are about to work out, something or
someone steps in and messes it all up?! I hate that.

This happens to you and me all the time, too. Just when we are about to have our
biggest breakthroughs, it seems like the heaviest burdens come rolling in.

We need a Distraction Detour.

1. STEP AWAY FOR A DAY

Once, I made a decision to cut out sugar completely from my life. But one day, I got
distracted and didn't even realize I was consuming a lot of sugar. The next morning
I woke up and my head hurt, my body ached, and I was grumpy. I remembered why
I had given up sugar in the first place. I think sometimes we just need to take a
step back and remember the why behind our decisions to stick a commitment out.

2. FIND YOUR FORWARD

We need stuff to look forward to. When life gets into the rut-cycle and we are just
doing the same things over and over, it's easy to want to give up on pursuing more.
Whether you are the setting mini-goals type person or you need a reward to look
forward to, set it! Mark it on the calendar! Do what you have to do to get there.

- Ruth had a distraction-detour too. Let's see what it was; read
  Ruth 3:14-18.

Once again, Naomi steps in and saves the day!

- What final instruction does Naomi give Ruth in verse 18?

Wait. Don't move. Keep your eyes forward but stand still.

As we get ready to head into our final week and our fifth habit, I don't want you to miss this because this is the place where I think 75 percent of us start to quit.

We've done all the right things.
We've accepted the assignment of refinement.
We've followed through despite how we feel.
We've stayed open to God's movement.
And for goodness sakes, we are giving others what we need.

But we haven't seen the right results … yet.

- This is hard and it's why I love the Quit Quitting Verse today, fill in the blanks:
  We do this by _____ our _____ on _____,
  the champion who initiates and _____ our faith.
  HEBREWS 12:2A [NLT]

Hebrews 12:2 describes where God preserves and perfects our obedience. I don't want you to miss this. Guess what the another word for *perfecter* is? Oh goodness, I'm so excited to share this with you.

It's *FINISHER!*

That's right. God is asking today if will you keep your eyes on Him and let *Him* finish this process for you?

- What are some doubts you have about this process of giving others what you need?

I promise, next week is going to be powerful as we press on through Habit Five and bring this whole thing home. We are going to FINISH STRONG.

Our fourth habit of the woman who doesn't quit is:

HABIT FOUR: SHE GIVES OTHERS WHAT SHE NEEDS.

Using our Q.U.I.T. Strategy, let's look back this week and see where God has taken us so far.

Q: QUESTIONS WE NEED TO ASK

- Moving forward, how will you choose to be emotionally generous?

- Who will challenge you the most as you live emotionally generous?

U: UNDERSTANDING THE WORD

- Why was Boaz at the threshing floor?

- What was the purpose of Ruth's visit?

I: INTO THE PROMISE

- Which of the Quit Quitting Verses spoke to you the most this week?

T: TURN SOMETHING AROUND

- That person whose name you wrote down above, go ahead and plan out a way you are going to be emotionally generous with him or her this week. Write down what you are going to do and then after you do it, write down what his or her reaction was.

1. Babe Ruth, as quoted on *Goodreads.com* (online) [cited 2 February 2016]. Available from the Internet: *https://www. goodreads.com/author/quotes/3916262.Babe_Ruth.*
2. "Winnowing," *The Holman Christian Standard Bible Dictionary.* (Nashville, TN: Holman Bible Publishers, 2003), 1675.

habit five

She

moves

— FORWARD —

IN FAITH.

Difficult things take a long time, impossible things a little longer.[1]

ANDRÉ A. JACKSON

WHAT TO READ THIS WEEK: RUTH 4:1-22

WARM THINGS UP

When you were little, who was someone you looked up to?

Describe your journey through this Bible study in three words.

What is a promise you feel God has given you for your life you are still waiting to see fulfilled?

WATCH

To hear more from Nicki, download the optional video bundle to view Week Six at *www.lifeway.com/5HabitsStudy.*

CREATE CONVERSATION

What is something you want to celebrate with your group that God did through this study for you personally?

Which of the habits do you feel like you will be applying to your life the most?

Who is someone God has called you to inspire not to give up?

What has been a turning point in your faith?

Fill in the blank: "My next step [in faith] is _____."

Video sessions available for purchase at *www.lifeway.com/5HabitsStudy.*

FOCUS BRINGS FREEDOM

QUIT QUITTING VERSE

So that you won't become lazy but will be imitators of those
who inherit the promises through faith and perseverance.
HEBREWS 6:12

A few months ago, my daughter's 4×800-meter relay team made it to the state championships. My daughter told me her only goal was to beat the team with the yellow uniforms.

Her competitive nature has at times thrown off her running ability, so I looked my girl in the eye and said, "Taylor, remember: Stay in your lane. Run hard. And pass the baton!" She nodded her head and took off.

And do you know what happened? Her team not only finished the race strong, but they beat the school record!

Focus brought her freedom.

HABIT FIVE: SHE MOVES FORWARD IN FAITH.

As we enter into our fifth and final habit, she moves forward in faith, there is a need for a high-level of focus. Of all the habits, this might be the most important for you and me. It's really the final step and push toward becoming a woman who completes her God-assignments.

Last week we were left on the edge of our seats to see how this situation with Boaz and this next man in line for Ruth was going to play out. We saw a huge shift in Naomi and now Ruth is in a holding pattern. She's waiting, but she is waiting with focus.

My friend, this is hard. When we are committed to sticking something out with God, there isn't a timeline He has to follow. He's not on a deadline and it's a complicated process.

And sometimes moving forward in faith means standing completely still. Which is where we are picking back up with Ruth. She's standing still. With her eyes on the end goal. The process is completely out of her hands now.

As Naomi said …

> Wait, my daughter, until you find out what happens. For
> the man will not rest until the matter is settled today.
> RUTH 3:18 [NIV]

She is correct. And just like Ruth is in a holding pattern, so is Boaz.

- Read Ruth 4:1-2. What does it say Boaz did in verse 1?
  □ Ran to find the other Kinsmen Redeemer
  □ Sat down at the gate
  □ Drove to his friend's house to hang out for the day

There is something so significant about Boaz "taking a seat" at the gate. The Hebrew word for *sat down* is *yashab*. It means *to sit, remain, dwell.*[2]

Boaz is not running around the town trying to find this guy. He's sitting, waiting patiently, and carefully planning out this process.

- Read 2 Chronicles 20:17. Where is God asking you to sit still right now?

- Read John 15:7. How is God showing you to remain in Him?

- Read Psalm 91:1. In what ways does your heart need to dwell in God's presence more?

I think one of the mistakes I make is believing moving forward in faith requires much movement on my part. Sure, there are times where God asks us to take huge leaps of faith with Him. But I'm finding there are a lot more days when my moving forward in faith means just being faithful in the day-in and day-out tasks of life.

It's hard to be faithful day after day after day. Taking a risk every now and then seems very doable for most people. But it's those people who get up each day and say, "Today is a day of moving forward in faith," and get the kids to school, clean the house, drive the carpool, go the extra mile at work, read their Bible, use their words carefully, and honor God with their simple steps that seem to have the greatest impact.

We have fooled ourselves into believing that serving God in a significant way means standing on a stage with lights, smoke, and skinny jeans.

- What are the two things that today's Quit Quitting Verse tells us to imitate after those who have gone before us?
  1.
  2.

Faith and perseverance go hand in hand. Sometimes perseverance just looks like where we see Boaz and Ruth today. Standing still. Waiting. Holding tight.

- What are some areas God is asking you to persevere through?

- In what situation are you still waiting to see the faithfulness of God to be revealed?

We are almost to the best part of this story and we are almost ready to see how all these habits combined are life changing. So sit tight [wink], keep going, and I'll see you on the next page as we see how the small steps we take keep our faith moving forward. Your focus through the rest of this process will bring you freedom!

UNLIKELY

QUIT QUITTING VERSE

Not that I have already reached the goal or am already
fully mature, but I make every effort to take hold of it
because I also have been taken hold of by Christ Jesus.
PHILIPPIANS 3:12

It was my senior year of high school. The grass was turning greener, birds were chirping louder, and department stores were lining their racks with beautiful formal gowns. Spring had sprung and that meant just one thing to a senior girl: prom.

Taking my seat in my homeroom class, I began working on the previous night's history assignment. The bell dinged and the redundant morning announcements blasted over the loudspeaker. I didn't pay much attention until I heard, "Today in every homeroom class you will need to nominate this year's prom king and queen."

Suddenly my stomach was tangled in knots. I knew never to get my hopes up. After all, I was the athletic girl who was at church every time the doors opened, not the socialite this honor required. While I knew not to expect it, inside I still wanted to be worthy of being prom queen.

I couldn't shake the dreadful feeling as sheets of paper were passed around the room for us write down our nominations. Would my name be on any of them?

It wouldn't take long to find out. Our teacher took his place, front and center of the classroom. As he collected the papers, he called out the names written down. I waited on pins and needles. Thirty seconds before the bell rang we'd nominated that year's prom king and queen.

Quickly I made my way to the only place a girl can get an ounce of privacy in a large high school: the bathroom. I shut the rusted stall door and wept.

It wasn't me … again. No one picked me. I was forever an unlikely prom queen candidate.

That moment was defining. Looking back, I can see that I started to become unlikely in a different way.

It could have ruined me—and in a way it did. For good. I discovered in Scripture there are many who didn't meet the qualifications of society; great heroes of faith who were unlikely candidates.

Moses was not an eloquent speaker, but he met with God and delivered the Ten Commandments to a generation of people (Ex. 19–20). David was an adulterer, but he is described as a man after God's heart (1 Kings 14:8). The Samaritan woman was a repeat sinner, but her testimony led her entire community to see Jesus (John 4).

God seemed to have handpicked and set apart these unlikely people. He used each of them for a redemptive purpose, despite their inadequacies. He turned their impossible to possible.

Which is exactly what God did for Ruth.

- Read Ruth 4:2-12. How many men did Boaz invite into this conversation?
  □ 2
  □ 19
  □ 10

- In verse 4, what is the first response of the kinsmen redeemer in regards to acquiring Ruth?

- What does Boaz tell him in verse 5 that makes him change his mind?

Boaz is not letting anyone stand in his way. For a moment, things got a little unsteady; this other redeemer decided he did want to take Ruth as his wife. Boaz had carefully thought this out and knew exactly what to say to this unnamed man.

- When was a time you didn't let anyone stand in your way to accomplish something?

- Fill in the blanks for today's Quit Quitting Verse:

    Not that I have _____ reached the _____ or am already
    fully _____, but I make every _____ to take hold of it because
    I also have been taken hold of by _____ _____.
    PHILIPPIANS 3:12 [HCSB]

- How is learning to have faith for the impossible part of our maturity process with God?

- Circle the reaction you tend to have when things aren't looking like they are going to work out:
  □ I don't know how to press on when things get messy.
  □ I tend to try for a little bit, but if it's too hard or complicated, I give up.
  □ I run strong toward what I want; no one is stopping me.

The King James version of Philippians 3:12 uses a phrase I want you to see.

    Not as though I had already attained, either were already
    perfect: but I follow after, if that I may apprehend that
    for which also I am apprehended of Christ Jesus.
    PHILIPPIANS 3:12 [KJV]

See where it says, "but I follow after"? I looked up the origin of this in the text in the Greek. The word is *dióko: to put to flight, pursue, by implication, to perse-cute.*[3] Moving forward in faith sometimes looks like standing still or waiting on God, and then other times it means putting things into action.

Boaz has put the impossible into action. And we are seeing the fulfillment of God's faithfulness through his faith.

Just like God showed me a powerful lesson through what it means for us or our situation to look unlikely in the eyes of the world, there are unlikely things He wants to show you right now too.

- What are some ways you feel unlikely or impossible for God to use?

Moving forward in faith is a call to persevere through the unlikely areas of life. You are growing, maturing, and developing into the woman God always knew you could be. Those who resist the unlikely places are the ones who often miss the greatest movements of God.

Boaz has taught us what it's like to look at a seemingly impossible situation and move forward in faith.

- Complete this sentence: I wish I had enough faith to _____.

- Read 1 John 5:5. Who is the only one who can help us overcome the world?

- Read Mark 10:52. What has the power to heal you?

- Read Romans 10:9. Have you confessed this with your mouth?

Someone once defined perseverance as long obedience in the same direction. This is what moving forward in faith really is. It's going to take time; it will be messy and unclear at times. But it's making the decision day after day, week after week, to trust and keep extending your faith to God.

FROM BROKEN TO BLESSED

QUIT QUITTING VERSE

But when you give to someone in need, don't let your left hand know what your right hand is doing. Give your gifts in private, and your Father, who sees everything, will reward you.
MATTHEW 6:3-4 [NLT]

Have you ever done something above and beyond while someone made you feel invisible?

My friend Monica had been volunteering at a church for a couple of weeks. Their receptionist was out on leave and she offered up her time to step in and help voluntarily. Day after day Monica showed up, smiled, answered the phones, and did whatever was needed while she was at the church office.

It was a small church and Monica had been part of it for several years so she was rather surprised one day when the phone rang and it was the pastor. He asked her to repeat her name when she answered the call. Even though Monica had served this church for quite some time, he had no idea who she was and began to intensely question her being there to answer the phones. Monica explained the situation and told him when the receptionist would be back.

It seemed as though no one had filled him in on Monica helping out with things in the absence of the secretary. Maybe he didn't intend to be rude, but Monica felt extremely small, unnoticed, and undervalued after she hung up the phone.

When she was telling me about this situation I felt really angry. Here she was helping out for free and all she got from the leader of this church was a rude phone call, not even a thank you?

Even though Boaz had noticed Ruth and had appreciated everything she had done for Naomi, I wonder if Ruth ever felt invisible? Just another anonymous face wandering through the fields?

- Have you ever felt like my friend Monica? Describe a time you have felt unseen:

- What are things people do to make us feel unseen?

- How good would you say you are at making people feel seen? Check your response.
  □ I am great at making other people feel seen.
  □ I need to work at noticing others.
  □ I'm pretty good but I could use some improvement.

The town knew she was a foreigner but how many people actually took the time to get to know Ruth? Was she ever discounted as a widow or just a woman with a hopeless situation?

Well, while throughout the story we didn't see many people take notice of Ruth, we know she was noticed here:

> The elders and all the people who were at the gate said,
> "We are witnesses. May the LORD make the woman who
> is entering your house like Rachel and Leah, who together
> built the house of Israel. May you be powerful in Ephrathah
> and famous in Bethlehem. May your house become like the
> house of Perez, the son Tamar bore to Judah, because of the
> offspring the LORD will give you by this young woman."
> RUTH 4:11-12

This blessing the elders give Boaz and Ruth is beautiful. They are saying, "Boaz, we believe in this situation. We want to see great things come from your life together."

Rachel and Leah had thirteen children between them. So for someone to put this blessing on Boaz and Ruth was quite the honor.

Because she has moved forward in faith, Ruth has gone from broken to blessed.

- Write out today's Quit Quitting Verses, Matthew 6:3-4.

- What are some of the things Ruth has done that have been "unseen"?

I think one of the cravings within every woman is the desire to be seen, to be noticed, and to be thanked for going above and beyond. I can promise you that on your way to becoming a woman who doesn't quit, God sees your faith. He sees the movement of your faith that is still, small, and even big.

And if you don't give up on this process with Him, I promise you will see His faithfulness fulfilled in your life too.

QUITTERS DON'T FINISH

**I have fought the good fight, I have finished
the race, I have kept the faith.**
2 TIMOTHY 4:7

That night I laid in my bed tossing and turning. I glanced at my phone … 11 P.M. …
1 A.M. … 3 A.M. … 5 A.M. The hours of the night passed and I found no sleep. I had
just made a big decision and was wrestling with a lot of doubt about it.

I decided it was time to quit something in my life.

Throughout the night one question continually tapped on my soul: "Did I really
do the right thing?" I just couldn't find the assurance my heart needed. Worry.
Anxiousness. Fear. And even a dose of sadness overcame me.

Sometimes it's so hard to know if we've made the right decision. I wish I could tell
you there's a perfect formula to follow to make sure you never quit a commitment
God's asking you to stick through again. While I don't have that promise to offer
you, God has shown me there's a difference between quitting and finishing.

That night, the peace of God washed over me as He showed me that particular
season was coming to a finish line for me. I wasn't quitting. I wasn't giving up.
I was finished.

Our Quit Quitting Verse today, 2 Timothy 4:7, gives us a clue into this process. For
some reason, when I read this verse I thought of running.

Let me clarify. I am so not a runner, but my husband Kris is. And I've noticed a
pattern with his running—it comes in seasons.

He's not always training for a marathon, and he's not always running a marathon. It comes in waves—train, run hard, finish. He doesn't always meet his goals, but he finishes his races. Then once he's rested and ready to start training again, he gets his shoes on and goes.

Life is filled with seasons in a similar pattern. There's a time to begin, there's a time to push hard, and there's a time to finish.

Quitting makes you say you're done because it's hard, you're tired, or you're frustrated. Finishing makes you say you're seeing this through until the end.

What does the end look like for you? Only God can show you that. But here is a great question to ask yourself as you consider finishing something:

- Has God found me faithful here so I can move there?

Here's the truth: quitters don't finish.

Quitters leave assignments, tasks, and relationships incomplete. Finishers follow through until the end.

- What is something in the past week you have finished? It could be anything from a load of laundry to a spreadsheet at work!

- What is something you plan on finishing this week but haven't yet?

- Looking back over your life, your seasons and your assignments, what are the things you have quit and what are the things you have finished?

THINGS I'VE QUIT	THINGS I'VE FINISHED

Seasons come and seasons go, but the faithfulness of our God remains the same, and so Ruth has learned. Now she is about to embark on a new season.

> Boaz took Ruth and she became his wife. When he was intimate with her, the LORD enabled her to conceive, and she gave birth to a son.
>
> RUTH 4:13

When I read this part of the story, I immediately thought of this verse:

> She who has believed is blessed because what was spoken to her by the Lord will be fulfilled!
>
> LUKE 1:45

Yes, moving forward in faith is trusting that eventually we will see the fulfillment of God's promises for us if we do not give up.

- Look up the following verses and write down what promise from God it offers our life:

  Matthew 11:28-29 holds a promise for _____.

  Romans 6:23 gives us the promise of _____.

  Revelation 21:4 offers a promise of _____.

I don't want you to hesitate in answering this next question. This is between you, me, and God. And since technically I can't see your response, I'm pretty much the safest person you know.

- What is a promise you feel like God has given you for your life?

I see some of you writing down promises for a husband, children, jobs, healthy marriages, friendships, and so many dreams. I know the older we get, the easier it is to give up on seeing the fulfillment of those things. But look …

> Then the women said to Naomi, "Praise the LORD, who has not
> left you without a family redeemer today. May his name become
> well known in Israel. He will renew your life and sustain you in
> your old age. Indeed, your daughter-in-law, who loves you and
> is better to you than seven sons, has given birth to him."
> RUTH 4:14-15

Naomi is seeing a new life before her. I know she would do anything to be back in the arms of her husband Elimelech. To hear the sound of her two boys running through the house again would make her heart overflow with joy. But she has found hope again.

A promise from God in the form of a marriage and a baby. It might not look how she dreamed, she might have fought every step of the way, and maybe some would even say she's too old to experience the faithfulness of God, but she did. And so will you.

FROM LOYALTY TO ROYALTY

QUIT QUITTING VERSE

Surprise! It's at the end.

My friend Lisa Allen is one of the wisest women I know. She's been a constant encouragement through my ministry assignments. In fact, there's a little bit of her love and encouragement sprinkled throughout this study.

Lisa always seems to know what I need to hear. So the other day while I was knee-deep in some God-assignments, she texted me to see how I was. I was honest with her and told her I was struggling. She texted back some of the most powerful, simple words someone has ever said to me:

I have enough faith for both of us.

I don't know where I'm leaving you on this journey, but I want to leave you with these words: I have enough faith for both of us. I believe together, we can and we will:

Accept our assignments of refinement. Follow through despite how we feel. Stay open to the movement of God. Give others what we need, and move forward in faith.

There's one last, really big, amazing thing we need to see from Ruth, this woman who didn't quit. Check out the Scripture below.

> "He shall be to you a restorer of life and a nourisher of your old age, for your daughter-in-law who loves you, who is more to you than seven sons, has given birth to him." Then Naomi took the child and laid him on her lap and became his nurse. And the women of the neighborhood gave him a name, saying, "A son has been born to Naomi." They named

him Obed. He was the father of Jesse, the father of David.
Now these are the generations of Perez: Perez fathered
Hezron, Hezron fathered Ram, Ram fathered Amminadab,
Amminadab fathered Nahshon, Nahshon fathered
Salmon, Salmon fathered Boaz, Boaz fathered Obed,
Obed fathered Jesse, and Jesse fathered David.

RUTH 4:15-22 [ESV]

Here's something you might not know about David. If we were to continue to look at his genealogy line, this is what we would see:

Abraham ... Isaac ... Jacob ... Judah ... Perez ... Hezron ... Aram ...

Amminadab ... Nahshon ... Salmon ... Boaz ... Obed by *Ruth* ... Jesse

... *David* ... Solomon ... Rehoboam ... Abijah ... Asa ... Jehoshaphat ...

Joram ... Uzziah ... Jotham ... Ahaz ... Hezekiah ... Manasseh ... Amon ...

Josiah ... Jechoniah ... Shealtiel ... Zerubbabel ... Abiud ... Eliakim ... Azor

... Zadok ... Achim ... Eliud ... Eleazar ... Matthan ... Jacob ... Joseph the

husband of Mary ... *Jesus* who is called the Messiah (Matt. 1:1-16).

Do you see it?! Look whose generational line God brought His one and only Son, Jesus Christ through! RUTH. Her loyalty led her to a generational line of kingdom royalty.

This makes me incredibly excited! Are there some generational lines you want to see changed in your family? Some patterns, behaviors, or addictions you want to change? Do you want to see God do miraculous things through YOU? Yes, yes, and yes!

These five habits we have learned from Ruth are life giving and life changing. We may not always get them just right. There may be times we are better at one habit more than the others. But if God did it for Ruth, He will do it for you and me.

I've been on this journey of following through with my commitments.

As I leave you my friend, this verse is my prayer for you to live out these five habits. It's our last Quit Quitting Verse.

> My counsel for you is simple and straightforward: Just go ahead with what you've been given. You received Christ Jesus, the Master; now live him. You're deeply rooted in him. You're well constructed upon him. You know your way around the faith. Now do what you've been taught. School's out; quit studying the subject and start living it! And let your living spill over into thanksgiving.
> COLOSSIANS 2:6-7 [MSG]

Go do miraculous things in Jesus' name!

For you always,

Nicki

Q.U.I.T. STRATEGY

Using our Q.U.I.T. Strategy, let's look back this week and see all the places where the assignment of refinement came into this story and ours.

Q: QUESTIONS WE NEED TO ASK

- How are you going to keep moving forward in faith?

U: UNDERSTANDING THE WORD

- What was the ultimate result of Ruth's obedience?

I: INTO THE PROMISE

- Which of the Quit Quitting Verses did you identify with most this week?

T: TURN SOMETHING AROUND

- We looked at so many different ways of moving forward in faith. Is God asking you to sit still or make movement right now? Write down what this looks like for you.

1. André A. Jackson, as quoted in *Chicken Soup for the Soul: Inspiration for the Young at Heart* (New York, NY: Simon and Schuster, 2011), 94.
2. "Hebrew Lexicon :: H3427 (KJV)." *Blue Letter Bible* (online) [cited 1 February 2016]. Available from the Internet: *http://www.blueletterbible.org*
3. "Greek Lexicon :: G1377 (KJV)." *Blue Letter Bible* (online) [cited 1 February 2016]. Available from the Internet: *http://www.blueletterbible.org*

Profile of Ruth

TIMELINE

ELIMELECH AND FAMILY
GO TO MOAB BECAUSE
OF THE FAMINE.

ELIMELECH DIES.

SONS MARRY
MOABITES.

SONS DIE.

RUTH & NAOMI GO
BACK TO BETHLEHEM.

RUTH MEETS BOAZ.

BOAZ PROVIDES FOR
RUTH & NAOMI.

RUTH APPROACHES BOAZ
AT THE THRESHING FLOOR.

BOAZ GOES TO THE CITY GATE.

BOAZ MARRIES RUTH.

RUTH GIVES
BIRTH TO OBED.

THE FIVE HABITS

One   SHE ACCEPTS THE
ASSIGNMENT OF
REFINEMENT.

two   SHE FOLLOWS THROUGH
DESPITE HOW SHE FEELS.

three   SHE STAYS OPEN
TO THE MOVEMENT
OF GOD.

four   SHE GIVES OTHERS
WHAT SHE NEEDS.

five   SHE MOVES FORWARD
IN FAITH.

FUN FACTS

- Ruth is in the lineage of Jesus.

- Bethlehem means "House of Bread."

- Moabites are descendants of Lot,
  Abraham's nephew (Gen. 19:30-38).

- Ruth lived during the time of the Judges.

- The Book of Ruth was read during Jewish
  festivals, particularly the Festival of Weeks.

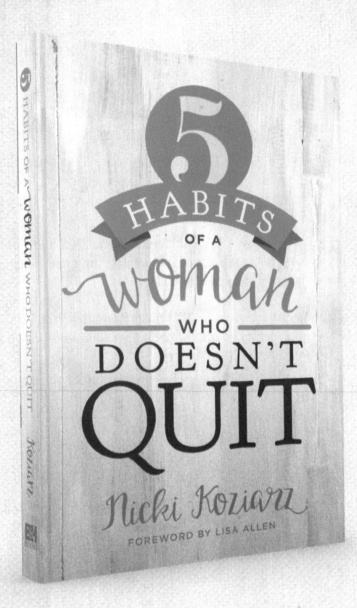

ABOUT PROVERBS 31 MINISTRIES

If you were inspired by *A Woman Who Doesn't Quit* and desire to deepen your own personal relationship with Jesus Christ, I encourage you to connect with Proverbs 31 Ministries.

Proverbs 31 Ministries exists to be a trusted friend who will take you by the hand and walk by your side, leading you one step closer to the heart of God through:

Free online daily devotions | First 5 app | Daily radio program

Books and resources | Online Bible Studies

COMPEL Writer Training: www.CompelTraining.com

To learn more about Proverbs 31 Ministries call 877-731-4663 or visit www.Proverbs31.org.

Proverbs 31
MINISTRIES

WWW.PROVERBS31.ORG

Proverbs 31 Ministries, 630 Team Rd., Suite 100, Matthews, NC 28105